# THE SPLENDID HUNDRED

*The True Story of Canadians Who Flew in
the Greatest Air Battle of World War II*

**Other Books by the Author**

THE COURAGE OF THE EARLY MORNING
COURAGE IN THE AIR: Canada's Military Heritage: Volume I
COURAGE ON THE BATTLEFIELD: Canada's Military Heritage: Volume II
COURAGE AT SEA: Canada's Military Heritage: Volume III

# THE SPLENDID HUNDRED

*The True Story of Canadians Who Flew in
the Greatest Air Battle of World War II*

*By*

## ARTHUR BISHOP

*Foreword by*
Lieutenant-General G. Scott Clements
Commander, Air Command

**McGraw-Hill Ryerson**
Toronto  Montreal

THE SPLENDID HUNDRED
Copyright © 1994 by Arthur Bishop

First published in 1994 by
McGraw-Hill Ryerson Limited
300 Water Street
Whitby, Ontario, Canada L1N 9B6

**Canadian Cataloguing in Publication Data**

Bishop, William Arthur, 1923-
  Splendid hundred: Canadian courage in the Battle of Britain

Includes bibliographical references and index.
ISBN 0-07-551683-7

1. Britain, Battle of, 1940. 2. World War, 1939–1945 – Aerial operations, Canadian. 3. Canada. Royal Canadian Air Force – History – World War, 1939–1945. 4. Fighter pilots – Canada. I. Title.

D756.5.B7B5 1994      940.54'4971      C94-930547-2

Photographs courtesy of John Grodzinski
Publisher: Donald S. Broad
Text design: Dianna Little
Cover design: Dave Hader/Studio Conceptions
Editorial services provided by Word Guild, Toronto

**Printed and bound in the United States**

To HARTLAND MOLSON
One of the magnificent "Few"
and a lifelong friend and supporter.
And, in anyone's log book,
a Canadian champion.

# ACKNOWLEDGEMENTS

My heartfelt thanks to the following for their assistance in various ways:

Cilla, my wife, tops the list. She initiated the idea, a *splendid* one, if I might add. She also helped with the organization and format of the project.

The Air Force Heritage Fund's assistance is greatly appreciated in making this work possible. Special thanks to Don Pearsons and his successor, Bill March, at Air Command Headquarters in Westwin, Manitoba.

Carl Christie, the Directorate of History's senior research officer, was his usual most helpful self in providing the D-Hist files and, in particular, the biographies of Battle of Britain pilots, which were most useful.

Anne Melvin, the Royal Canadian Military Institute's librarian, whose help and enthusiasm, as in the course of two earlier books, is highly appreciated. Thanks also to the RCMI for the use of their very fine library.

John Grodzinski, researcher and historian, and an able writer in his own right, for his aid in many ways but particularly in digging up Battle of Britain statistics and combat reports, as well as a wealth of other material.

G. Scott Clements, Commander of Air Command, who generously consented to author the Foreword to this book.

Don Broad, my publisher, and the staff at McGraw-Hill Ryerson, and Don Loney, my editor, for their enthusiasm and encouragement.

Shirley Corriveau, for a superb job of copy editing.

# TABLE OF CONTENTS

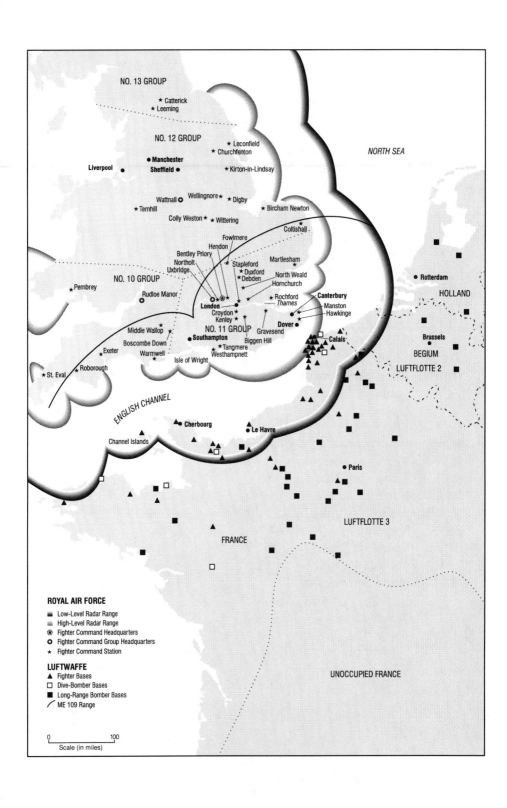

NO. 13 GROUP

★ Catterick
★ Leeming

NO. 12 GROUP

★ Leconfield
★ Churchfenton

● Manchester
Liverpool    Sheffield ●    ★ Kirton-in-Lindsay
        ●

Wattnall ⊙  Wellingnore ★  ★ Digby
★ Ternhill
    Colly Weston ★  ★ Wittering
                Fowlmere
            Hendon
        Bentley Priory
        Northolt
        Uxbridge
    NO. 10 GROUP        ★ Stapleford
                ★ ★ Duxford
                ★ Debden
★ Pembrey                    North Weald
                        Hornchurch
        Rudloe Manor ⊙
                ★ Rochford
London ⊙⊛ ★        Thames
    Croydon ★    ★ Canterbury
    Kenley ★        Manston
                    Hawkinge
    Middle Wallop ★ ★        Dover ●
                Gravesend
Boscombe Down ● Southampton    Biggin Hill
    Exeter ★        ★ Tangmere
    Warmwell ★    ★ Westhampnett
        Isle of Wright
★ St. Eval
★ Roborough

NORTH SEA

★ Bircham Newton
Coltishall
Martlesham ★

● Rotterdam
HOLLAND

● Brussels
BEGIUM
LUFTFLOTTE 2

ENGLISH CHANNEL

Calais □

▲ Cherbourg    ● Le Havre

Channel Islands

● Paris

LUFTFLOTTE 3

FRANCE

**ROYAL AIR FORCE**
▨ Low-Level Radar Range
▨ High-Level Radar Range
⊛ Fighter Command Headquarters
⊙ Fighter Command Group Headquarters
★ Fighter Command Station

**LUFTWAFFE**
▲ Fighter Bases
□ Dive-Bomber Bases
■ Long-Range Bomber Bases
╱ ME 109 Range

UNOCCUPIED FRANCE

0        100
Scale (in miles)

# ABBREVIATIONS

| | |
|---|---|
| **AOC** | Air Officer Commanding |
| **BCATP** | British Commonwealth Air Training Plan |
| **CAF** | Canadian Air Force |
| **CO** | Commanding Officer |
| **DFC** | Distinguished Flying Cross |
| **Do** | Dornier |
| **E/A** | Enemy Aircraft |
| **F/L** | Flight Lieutenant |
| **F/O** | Flying Officer |
| **F/S** | Flight-Sergeant |
| **He** | Heinkel |
| **Ju** | Junkers |
| **Me** | Messerschmitt |
| **OKW** | *Oberkommando Wehrmacht* (German Military High Command) |
| **Ops** | Operations |
| **P/O** | Pilot Officer |
| **RAE** | Royal Aircraft Establishment |
| **RAF** | Royal Air Force |
| **RCAF** | Royal Canadian Air Force |
| **RFC** | Royal Flying Corps |
| **R/T** | Radio Transmitter |
| **Sgt** | Sergeant |
| **S/L** | Squadron Leader |
| **TAF** | Tactical Air Force |
| **W/C** | Wing Commander |

# FOREWORD

The Battle of Britain has long been recognized as the pre-eminent air battle of the modern era. From July 10 to October 31, 1940, the German Luftwaffe tried unsuccessfully to take control of the skies over England as a prelude to invasion. They were thwarted in their attempt by a handful of young men, drawn from many different nations, whose exploits have become legendary.

During the summer of 1940, Canada furnished a large number of young men who served in the Royal Air Force as well as a Royal Canadian Air Force squadron. However, very little attention has been devoted to Canadian participation in the Battle of Britain. Arthur Bishop, a Second World War Spitfire pilot, rectifies this omission by chronicling the achievements of the Canadians who flew during those fateful months. He weaves a solid tale of tragedy and heroism that brings the reader into the cockpit, sharing the confidence of veteran pilots and the uncertainty of fledgling aviators experiencing combat for the first time. It is a story worth reading.

The Battle of Britain is a part of the history and heritage of the air force and of Canada. The record of courage and sacrifice that was written by Canadians in the skies over England is a precious legacy that has been passed down to the young men and women of today's Air Command. The effect that a few dedicated individuals can have on the course of history is a valuable lesson to all Canadians as they face the challenges of an uncertain world.

G. Scott Clements, CMM, CD
Lieutenant-General
Commander, Air Command

*Whoever among us longs for a quiet life has certainly chosen the wrong epoch.*

Leon Trotsky

*Very few and very weary . . .*

John Milton

# CHAPTER ONE

# SCRAMBLE

For Johnny Kent of Winnipeg, Tuesday the first of October, 1940, dawned as just another day to wait for the call to combat. Nothing special. Routine, actually. In fact, on this particular cloudy morning Northolt aerodrome in Middlesex, only fourteen miles west of London, pretty well typified the deceptively relaxed state of vigilance of the thirty-three Royal Air Force fighter fields spread across southeast England. Wearing bright yellow Mae West life-preservers over their blue uniforms, pilots lazed about their dispersal huts dozing, chatting, playing cards, writing letters, listening to phonograph records, killing time. But under that outward display of calm lay an inner nervousness, an itching for action to which they would instantly respond once the signal came to "scramble" — take off on the double and intercept the enemy. With the help of their ground crews, who stood by their Hawker Hurricane or Supermarine Spitfire fighter planes, the pilots had the drill down cold. When the order came, they would dash to their aircraft while pulling on their parachute seat packs, climb up on the port wing root and lower themselves into the cockpit. Then donning their leather flying helmets that dangled from the control column, they would plug their facemasks into the radio transmitter, which would simultaneously connect them to the oxygen feed. Next step, pull down the goggles strapped to the helmet. That accomplished they would "press tits" (punch ignition buttons with index and forefingers) bringing the Rolls-Royce Merlin engine to life while the "erks" (ground crews) secured their safety straps. From the time the phone jangled and the Klaxon horn began its mournful wail, they could be airborne within three minutes. In pilots' lexicon, "A piece of cake!"

At Northolt this day, the summons did not arrive until mid-afternoon when the cathode tube screens at the chain of radar stations picked up blips indicating a large formation of aircraft approaching the Sussex coast from across the English Channel. As he raced for his Hurricane, Johnny

Kent had no inkling that he was about to become embroiled in the most spectacular dogfight of that Homeric encounter of the Second World War — the Battle of Britain.

By mid-September, the German night Blitz on London had taken its toll on civilian life, driving people into the Underground and setting entire city blocks ablaze. During the day, the German air force continued its raids of large gaggles of twin-engine bombers escorted by single-engine Messerschmitt 109 fighters, keeping the Allied fighter pilots as busy as they had been all summer. And not only were the latter frequently outnumbered but, where the Hurricane was concerned, a bit outclassed. Unlike the all-metal Messerschmitt — and Spitfire — the Hurricane was a stopgap between the old biplane and the new monoplanes. Its construction was part metal, part fabric. That gave it one advantage, however; it made it easy to repair.

Though the differences in performance were marginal, they were significant. The "Em-ee" had a flat and level speed of more than 300 miles an hour; the "Hurrie" somewhat under that. Many of the German fighters were armed with nose-firing cannon, while the British fighters, including the Spitfires, were equipped with the less powerful Browning machinegun. The Messerschmitt could outdive and outclimb the Hurricane, but the Hawker fighter held the edge in a dogfight because of its tighter turning capacity. Still, although the Hurricane could hold its own, it was no proper match for the Me 109 except in the hands of an expert. It was for these reasons that the Hurricanes were usually assigned the role of engaging the slower flying bombers while the faster, higher-altitude Spitfires tackled the enemy fighters. On this occasion, however, the orders called for a slight deviation from that strategy. Kent's 303 Polish Squadron was assigned to attack the bombers while No. 1 Royal Canadian Air Force Squadron, another fighter outfit stationed at Northolt that was also equipped with Hurricanes, was to provide protective cover from the German fighters.

All of this on October 1, 1940, was shortly to have a sharp bearing on the action about to take place. At this moment, however, Kent had to concentrate solely on getting his fighter off the ground and ready to do battle. As soon as his aircraft lifted into the air, in a sweeping motion he pulled the cockpit canopy shut, shifted the control column from his left hand to his right and jammed the undercarriage selector forward to lift the wheels. Then, transferring the stick back to his right hand, he flipped a switch to close the flaps. Next he turned the gun-button on. This completed, all in a matter of seconds, he pushed his radio transmitter forward and, through his face-microphone, casually announced:

"Apathy Leader [his call sign] to Grata [ground controller] — Airborne! Over." Pulling back the ratchet-like apparatus to the "receive" position, his earphones crackled with the reply: "Grata to Apathy Leader. Understood! Out."

By the time he had climbed to 10,000 feet and advised the controller he had reached "Angels Ten," Kent had spotted the enemy formation. Making a wide turn to set up to attack the bombers, he watched warily as the Messerschmitt cover appeared above him. In so doing, however, he had outdistanced his own squadron. Meanwhile, the Canadians, who had been bounced by another formation of fighters, were forced to break in the opposite direction. But, because both squadrons were on different radio frequencies, neither could tell the other what it was up to. To make matters worse, with the impending encounter, his own pilots forgot to speak English and began nattering over the radio transmitter (R/T) in Polish which "Kentowski," despite the nickname they had bestowed upon him, could not understand. Suddenly, their flight commander found himself out on a limb, all alone.

Kent's troubles were only beginning, however. As he swept in to open fire his ring-and-bead gunsight filled, not with bombers, but the wily Me 109s. Singling out one of them and taking aim, a stream of tracer bullets suddenly streaked past him from behind leaving trails of white smoke in their wake. Glancing through his rearview mirror atop the windscreen as he took evasive action, he saw the ugly yellow snout of the vaunted German fighter. But by this time his instincts and experience as an air-fighter had taken over.

To the surprise of the German pilot, Kent broke into a hard, steep climbing turn to the right. Because virtually all crankshafts in single-engine fighters rotated clock-wise, the torque they created made a turn to the left easier and more natural. For that reason, Kent always broke in the opposite direction; it was unexpected. It upset the attacker's automatic reaction. And in this case, that split-second got Kent out of a very twitchy spot.

But his predicament was far from over; he found himself in the midst of a hornet's nest of enemy fighters. If he tried to dive away, he would be easy prey before he could reach the cloud cover below. He had to stay and fight. Keeping his Hurricane in a steady, steep, right-hand turn, he applied enough rudder so that it skidded, making it a difficult target for the Me 109s that dove from above and attacked from below. His tactic succeeded; not one of the enemy had a strike.

When the bullets stopped flying by him, Kent momentarily straightened out and, as four Messerschmitts banked in front of him, he let go a quick burst that sent one of them spiralling down, pouring smoke. Then, when the Germans milled around him again, he yanked his aircraft into a skidding right-hand turn once more.

In one way, Kent had the upper hand; he could fire at anything that flew across his path, and the Germans had difficulty staying out of each other's way. When one of them appeared fifty yards in front of his nose, he opened fire, his bullets finding the mark. The Messerschmitt burst into flames and disappeared. Kent immediately swung into a turn as the enemy planes launched another attack. At that moment the German leader pulled up and rolled underneath him. Kent reversed direction, got below the belly of the Messerschmitt and let fly a short burst. Strikes were visible all along the fuselage, but before he could fire again, the enemy fighters started to climb away.

Their retreat was not necessarily the consequence of being outfought by a single British fighter, although that might have shaken their confidence or at least amazed them. The Messerschmitt had limited endurance. This was one of the chief factors favouring the Royal Air Force (RAF) in the Battle of Britain. The Me 109's fuel supply lasted little more than an hour which restricted its depth of penetration over England and minimized the time it could spend in combat.

As the German fighters hightailed it towards France, Kent followed but was unable to catch them. Halfway across the Channel, he turned back. However, he did manage to make a count: thirty-eight in all which, added to the two he had destroyed or probably shot down, meant he had been up against odds of forty-to-one. But he wasn't quite through yet. On his way back to the English coast he met a lone 109 heading home which he fired at but with no result; the enemy dove into a cloud before Kent got another shot at it. Probably just as well, for he had spent the last of his ammunition. Thus ended one of the most incredible aerial duels in combat history. Not only had Kent shot down one aircraft, he had probably destroyed a second and damaged another in the most mismatched dogfight of the war. In an aircraft definitely inferior to the enemy planes, he had escaped without a scratch; not a single bullet or shell had hit his Hurricane.

Kent's feat epitomized the role of the hundred Canadians who fought in the Battle of Britain. They were an extraordinarily high-spirited band always keen to come to grips with the enemy — so much so that they scored more victories per pilot than any other Allied group during that historic encounter. This is their story.

# CHAPTER TWO

# THE FIRST OF OUR FEW

Though Johnny Kent ran a close second, Canada's most experienced pilot in the Battle of Britain was a short, stocky individual from Rosthern, Saskatchewan. While Kent been engaging forty-plus German fighters, Ernie McNab led the first Canadian fighter squadron in another mêlée with the Messerschmitts. His flying experience went back to the mid-1920s; while attending university, he took pilot training with the Royal Canadian Air Force during the summers. On graduating as a civil engineer, he decided to make the service his career instead. When he joined the RCAF in 1928 it was merely four years old and consisted of slightly more than 100 officers and 300 other ranks. Its duties primarily were civil and included aerial surveying, mapping, forestry and fisheries patrols, exploration, experimental flights, transportation, rescue work, medical missions and carrying mail. McNab carried out all of these exercises as well as completing a stint as an instructor.

In 1932, personnel were slashed by 108 to 178 officers and 591 men as a consequence of the Depression. McNab survived the cut, a testimony to his exceptional skills as an airman. He had already proved to be one of the air force's outstanding pilots and had been one of three selected as a member of the élite Siskin Flight, Canada's first aerobatic team which in 1930 and 1931 toured Canada and the United States.

Johnny Kent would like to have joined the RCAF as well. But because enrollment had to be restricted for budgetary purposes, the qualifications were of such high standards that they ruled out any chance of eligibility for the tall Winnipegger, as they did for many other young Canadians who wanted to become military pilots. The requirements called for at least a college degree, and even at that there was no guarantee an applicant would be accepted.

Kent had been bitten by the flying bug early in life. In 1929, when he was fifteen years old, his father arranged for him to go up in a Gypsy

Moth at the Winnipeg Flying Club. Two years later, when Kent had passed his senior matriculation, his father paid for his flying lessons. By November 1931, he was awarded his Private Pilot's Licence No. 919 to become, at seventeen, the youngest licensed pilot in Canada. Later he resigned from the flying club to join a mercantile aviation enterprise where, in 1933, he received his licence qualifying him as the youngest Canadian commercial pilot.

Another Canadian flyer of note who had also been scrambled from Northholt that October afternoon in 1940 was Gordie McGregor of Montreal, then a flight commander with No. 1 RCAF Squadron. Though he did not possess quite the experience in the air that Kent or McNab had, in the mid-1930s he had set an enviable record as a Canadian pilot.

McGregor learned to fly in Ontario, at the Kingston Flying Club. But unlike Kent or McNab, he was strictly an amateur and flying was primarily a pastime. He was employed by the Bell Telephone Company, where he held the position of district manager. However, he became so adept at his sideline that between 1935 and 1938 he won the Webster Trophy, awarded annually to the outstanding Canadian amateur pilot, three times.

Another outstanding flyer with No. 1 RCAF Squadron that first day in October 1940 was Deane Nesbitt, who learned to fly on Tiger Moths and Fleets in 1935 at the Montreal Light Aeroplane Club. Like his cohort McGregor, Nesbitt fitted the "Sunday Flyer" category. He held a post with the family financial institution, Nesbitt and Thompson.

Just as Kent had done, Howard Blatchford, who later became known as "Cowboy" Blatchford, began taking an interest in flying in his teens. The son of a former Edmonton mayor and Member of Parliament, he obtained his pilot's licence in 1930 and had his heart set on joining the RCAF. However, like so many others he could not meet the entrance requirements. He decided to bide his time and, for the next five years, flew as a bush pilot.

During the summer of 1931, Vaughan Corbett of Montreal, who was attending Royal Military College (RMC) in Kingston, took advantage of the air force's provisional pilot officer course and trained at Camp Borden. He did not go directly into the RCAF, though he hovered on the fringe. After graduating with a law degree from McGill University, he became assistant secretary of the Canadian Aviation Insurance Managers in Montreal.

On graduating from RMC in 1928, Hartland Molson, who worked for the family brewery, Molson's of Canada, became a member of the Army Militia with which he served until 1933. But by then friends, including Deane Nesbitt, had sparked his interest in flying. He quickly became one of the Montreal flying club's keenest members.

*        *        *

At 11:00 p.m. on Monday, July 31, 1934, at Westminster, in the face of the growing might of the new German Luftwaffe, the British House of Commons voted 404 to 60 to increase the number of Royal Air Force squadrons by forty-nine over the next five years. Aircrews were now needed in a hurry. The service quickly launched a campaign to enlist recruits from Great Britain and the Commonwealth. In Canada the response, in two cases at least, was almost immediate.

By 1935, more funds became available for the RCAF and the service was being re-equipped with more modern aircraft. But it hadn't changed the enrollment standards. Johnny Kent had almost given up hope of a military career as a lost cause when he came across an RAF advertisement in *The Aeroplane* offering short service commissions of six years' duration. He immediately applied and shortly afterwards received notification advising him to report to Winnipeg for a medical examination and an interview. This happened four times, and Kent became so fed up he wrote back telling them to withdraw his application and return his papers. To his astonishment, back came a reply saying that he had been selected and was to report at his own expense to the British Air Ministry in London. But the order made it explicit that His Majesty's Government would be under no obligation in the event the RAF failed to accept him. Kent's family decided to take the risk and provided him with funds to make the journey. In February 1935, Kent sailed for England with high hopes of being accepted as a fighter pilot.

Cowboy Blatchford wasn't long in following in Kent's prop-wash. After five years of bush-piloting, he decided he'd had enough of commercial flying. Early in 1935, he too boarded a ship bound for England to join the British air service. Unlike Kent, however, Blatchford had his heart set on becoming a bomber pilot.

# CHAPTER THREE

# THE FOLLOWERS

By 1936, Canadians were enthusiastically applying for RAF commissions. More than fifty applicants from all walks of life and varied backgrounds, and for myriad different reasons, sailed to England — at their own expense — to enlist. Doug Christie of Westmount had just graduated from McGill University; Bill Nelson and Joe Laricheliere represented French and English Canada from Montreal; John Boyle came from Casselman, Ont.; Lionel Gaunce from Lethbridge had been a former corporal in the Edmonton Militia Regiment; Robert "Butch" Barton, from Kamloops, B.C., had given up his job as a bank teller; and Mark "Hilly" Brown of Portage la Prairie, like Cowboy Blatchford and Johnny Kent, just wanted to fly.

Kent had picked the right vocation. At the end of his military pilot training on Avro Tudors at Sealand in England, he graduated as the only pilot to be assessed as "exceptional," having also won the silver trophy for the most proficient student at forced-landing procedures. "The only cup I ever won," he would remark later. Kent's was the last initial training class undertaken by the RAF Training Command within the service. Expansion had resulted in the utilization of facilities offered by civilian flying schools, and this allowed for greater and faster growth. The hopeful pilots, on their way from Canada and other members of the Commonwealth, were welcomed with open arms.

At home in Canada, the expansion of the RCAF also got underway. This included plans for the formation of No. 1 Fighter Squadron. Stationed at Trenton, Ont., it was to be equipped with the Armstrong-Whitworth Siskin fighter, no stranger to Ernie McNab who was to become one of the unit's flight commanders. The squadron's first diary entry read: "Routine flight duties." No mucking around with details there.

The RCAF also formed the Auxiliary Squadrons, a direct outgrowth of the Non-Permanent Active Air Force established in 1932. One of them,

No. 115 at Cartierville Airport, attracted members of the Montreal Light Aeroplane Club, among them Deane Nesbitt, Hartland Molson, Vaughan Corbett, Paul Pitcher, a young Montreal lawyer, and Dal Russel of Toronto, who had left school to take a job as a salesman with a Quebec industrial firm.

The following year, 1937, saw enlistments in the permanent RCAF open up to a small degree. One of the enrollers was Eric Beardmore, who joked that he had inkling of what was in store. "After all, I was born in Berlin," he told the recruiting officer. Educated in Montreal and Ottawa, after five years in the non-permanent militia, the Victoria Rifles, he decided to make the air force his career. About the same time, Jean Desloges, a graduate of the University of Ottawa and a former Mountie, joined the service. Other enrollers of that ilk were George Hyde of Westmount and Thomas Harnett from Moncton.

When Peter O'Brian of Toronto graduated from Varsity, he decided to make the air force his career. He knew advancement in the RCAF would be slow and limited, so he applied for a permanent commission in the RAF. Having been accepted, he reported to Cranwell Military College.

On arrival in England, Hilly Brown, who had begun flying training as a teenager in Manitoba, quickly established his remarkable skill as a pilot, completing his initial training with exceptionally high marks: 875 out of a possible 1,000. At the end of February, he was posted to No. 1 Fighter Squadron RAF stationed at Tangmere on the Sussex coast. By this time, he had logged 150 flying hours.

Having completed a stint with 19 Squadron RAF at Duxford, flying Gloucester Gauntlet biplanes — the latest and fastest British fighter at the time — Johnny Kent, after a leave in Canada, joined the Royal Aircraft Establishment (RAE) at Farnborough as a test pilot.

That year, the British Air Ministry had been busy making plans for the organization of an Empire Training Scheme. This was an immense undertaking, and because of Canada's safe distance from a potential European war zone, it was a natural place to implement the scheme. But, although both Australia and New Zealand enthusiastically endorsed the plan, it ran into strong headwinds — political ones.

Prime Minister Mackenzie King nixed the notion — for the time being, anyway. Electorally, a home defence posture was more acceptable with a long-range view of having an autonomous Canadian air force overseas. This posture won strong support in many RCAF circles.

In 1938, the year of the Austrian *Anschluss* and the Munich crisis, Nazi Germany's intentions became crystal clear. Canadian plans for expansion of the RCAF began speeding up, and behind the scenes renewed efforts were made to launch what had now become on paper the British Empire Training Plan. New equipment was on order. Meanwhile, the RAF was making up for lost time by arming its squadrons with modern monoplane fighters and more pilots. The exodus of Canadians to obtain short service commissions in the British service continued, with the blessing of the RCAF which helped process the candidates before they shipped overseas — still at their own expense.

Among this group were British-born Stan Turner, who had been studying engineering at the University of Toronto; Ian "Duke" Arthur of Fort Garry; Robert "Slim" Grassick of London; and John Latta of Victoria, a former salmon fisherman.

That same year, Gordie McGregor was transferred into a senior position with Bell Telephone at the company's head office in Montreal. He wasted no time joining 115 Auxiliary Squadron.

Like Eric Beardmore and others at home, Ed Reyno decided to enlist in the RCAF. He had all the qualifications. A native of Halifax, he had received his bachelor's degree from St. Mary's University. About the same time, Thomas Little of Montreal also enrolled.

By 1939, the clouds of war hung heavy over Europe. But before Hitler invaded Poland, two of the future Canadian Few had already distinguished themselves. Johnny Kent's job with the Experimental Section of the Royal Aircraft Establishment had been to test aerial balloon cable-cutting devices. It meant that a bomber could fly into a balloon barrage and, by means of blades affixed to the nose of the aircraft, could knife its way through. This was exacting work, not to mention dangerous. But Kent became so proficient at the assignment and achieved such worthwhile results he was awarded the Air Force Cross. At the same time he was also given a permanent RAF commission which in peacetime meant a quicker chance of promotion. At Cranwell, Peter O'Brian attained such high marks and standing that he became the first — and only — Canadian ever to be awarded the coveted Sword of Honour.

Cowboy Blatchford's hopes of becoming a bomber pilot were soon dashed. Because of the high marksmanship he displayed at aerial gunnery, he was assigned to fighters. He found himself a member of 41 Squadron RAF, then stationed at Catterick in Yorkshire, equipped with Hawker Furies. Butch Barton was also posted to the same outfit.

*          *          *

In January 1939, 41 Squadron was refitted with Supermarine Spitfires. This legend among all fighter aircraft was revolutionary, built of an all-metal design except for the ailerons, rudder and elevators, and possessing the classic elliptical mainplanes that became its trademark. Able to reach 355 miles an hour and climb to 34,000 feet, the aircraft's design was to demonstrate later that it could attain a Mach 1 or 2 rating — an ability to fly through the sound barrier. An aircraft ahead of its time. As members of the squadron, Cowboy Blatchford and Butch Barton were among the first Canadians to fly the famous airplane. Their unit would be assigned to guard the Royal Naval fleet at Scapa Flow on the east coast of Scotland.

When Duke Arthur graduated from the White Waltham Training School, he was posted to No. 3 Air Observer School at Aldergrove in Northern Ireland. There he flew the lumbering Hereford bombers which had been taken out of operational service for some time. It was tiresome work, boring in fact, but Arthur showed an "above average" aptitude.

In his native city of Edmonton, Willie McKnight had served in the army militia from 1935 to 1938. During part of that time he attended medical school at the University of Alberta. Then, early in 1939, on impulse he decided to drop his studies and sail to England to join the RAF. After being accepted, he made up his mind to continue to study medicine at Edinburgh once the war was over. It was a vow he would never keep.

McKnight was one of the later and last Canadians to enlist in the program to award RAF short service commissions — what had become expanded into the Direct Entry Scheme. Over a twelve-month period, a total of 118 Canadians had journeyed to Great Britain to enroll.

In February, seven Hurricanes were crated and shipped from England to Vancouver. There they were assembled and flown to Calgary where No. 1 Squadron RCAF was based. Thus Ernie McNab became one of the first to fly the new single-wing fighters. These were Mark 1's, with two-bladed propellers capable of 320 miles an hour flat and level, a service ceiling of 34,000 feet and a range of 500 miles.

Hilly Brown, whose No. 1 RAF Squadron had been equipped with Hurricanes in October of the previous year, wrote home in March: "I have been reading a lot about political history lately, and I feel sure there will be a war. It does not matter when it comes. The big thing will be that it must last long enough to bankrupt all countries, so that people will get a new deal when it is over." By this time Brown had logged more than 500 flying hours and was assigned to training new pilots as they joined the unit.

Peter O'Brian had been posted to 26 Squadron at Catterick. But, unlike the other squadron there — 41, in which Blatchford and Barton were flying Spitfires — O'Brian was assigned to army cooperation work flying Lysanders with 26 Squadron. These were slow, high-wing monoplanes that could take off and land in a minimum of space. O'Brian showed such aptitude to squadron life that he soon became the unit's adjutant.

It was late in the game, but having been accepted by the RAF, on August 4 "Skeets" Ogilvie of Ottawa gave up his job as a cashier and sailed for England aboard the SS *Letitia*. Ten days later he began his initial flight training at Hatfield. By that time Hitler had decided to invade Poland. The target date: September 1. Then, on August 23, Germany signed a non-aggression pact with Russia allowing her to make war with France and Britain.

As the RAF came to a state of readiness, the RCAF got set to go on a war footing. On August 25, at Calgary, all leaves and passes for No. 1 Squadron were cancelled. Five days later its seven Hurricanes, which had been crated, were loaded onto railway boxcars. Next day, on the eve of the Nazi invasion of Poland, the squadron proceeded east to take up headquarters at St. Hubert, outside of Montreal.

# CHAPTER FOUR

# PRESENCE

Cowboy Blatchford became the first Canadian fighter pilot in the Second World War to fire his guns in anger. At mid-afternoon on October 17, 1939, he shared in the destruction of a twin-engine German Heinkel 111 bomber. While leading a section of three Spitfires on convoy patrol at 10,000 feet over England's east coast near Whitby, one of his pilots spotted the enemy aircraft and made the first pass. Instead of taking evasive action, however, the German pilot tried to escape by diving to the deck. After a second pilot in the section gave chase, Blatchford pulled up astern of the Heinkel from 200 feet below and opened fire at 400 yards' range. But he came in too fast and had to climb quickly to avoid a collision.

He attacked again, once more from 400 yards. This time he slowed his speed and easily hit the target. Then one of the other members of the section finished the bomber off. The Heinkel burst into flames and the pilot ditched it in the sea where both he and his gunner were picked up by a British air-sea rescue launch. This marked the first World War II victory for 41 Squadron, and Blatchford's combat report was the first submitted by a Canadian in the conflict.

The first Canadian fighter pilot to experience enemy anti-aircraft fire was Johnny Kent, though technically it was not in a combat role. When the war started, Kent had reported to the Photographic Development Unit at Heston where he was assigned high-altitude photographic reconnaissance duties. The long-range Spitfires flown by the unit were stripped of all unnecessary weight, including armour and armament, to allow for an extra fuel tank and permit higher speeds.

On his first flight over Germany, Kent had just crossed the border at 20,000 feet when he heard a thumping noise that seemed to come from the aft section of the aircraft. As he flew on, the thumping got louder and the aircraft started to rock.

Judging that he might have to come down or bail out, as he turned back he discovered the trouble: German flak was bursting all around him. Kent proceeded to take evasive action to throw off the German gunners' aim. He then made a photographic run over his target as quickly as he could and headed home. "This first experience came as a distinct shock," he admitted later.

On September 8, as a member of No. 1 Squadron RAF, Hilly Brown flew with the unit from Tangmere to the French port of Le Havre. There the Hurricanes circled and then headed inland to Octeville aerodrome where they landed. As a member of the British Advanced Air Striking Force, Brown became the first Canadian airman to land in France in World War II.

These accomplishments were well worthy of the proud tradition set by their predecessors in World War I. But a Canadian identity was lacking. Canadian fighter pilots were scattered among more than sixty British squadrons. Riffling through family files, I found a document written in 1918 by my father, then Major William Avery Bishop, RAF. It read:

> Under the present circumstances, Canadians in the RAF, although doing remarkably well, are certainly not doing as well as if they were in a Canadian Corps for the reasons that (1) They are in a great many circumstances working under senior officers who do not understand them. (2) They are also working with officers who do not understand them or often appreciate their different point of view. (3) They have not the personal touch with their country which branches of the Canadian Corps have and consequently are not inspired by direct connection with the country they are fighting for and the people at home.

That view applied and prevailed just as strongly and importantly in 1939 as it had a generation earlier. In 1918, it resulted in the creation of the Canadian Air Force and the formation of the first two Canadian squadrons. At the beginning of the Second World War, it manifested itself in the materialization of a Canadianized RAF squadron. The subject arose and came to a head during negotiations over the British Commonwealth Air Training Plan which the British government presented to the Commonwealth nations on September 28, 1939. Mackenzie King had reversed his attitude towards the scheme. In 1937 he had rejected it; now he embraced it as a great opportunity politically and a giant step militarily. He saw Canada's primary wartime role as one to be fought in the air. Still, the early discussions at times were somewhat strained.

The British insisted that the BCATP take priority over all other Canadian military plans and at the same time asked that a RCAF squadron be dispatched overseas "at the earliest possible date." The Canadian De-partment of National Defence balked at the request, arguing that with the onus placed on it to implement the BCATP — an estimated 40,000 personnel would be needed — any major overseas commitment by the RCAF would so weaken it that the plan would be strangled at birth. But the Canadian government did want an early air force presence over-seas. Some sort of compromise was needed. This the British finally ac-cepted and out of an exchange of ideas evolved the concept of forming an RAF squadron made up of Canadian pilots already serving with the British.

On October 30, a seaplane squadron that had been abandoned in 1919 was resurrected as 242 (Canadian) Squadron RAF. To get things rolling, on November 1 at Church Fenton in Yorkshire, an RCAF exchange officer acting as CO and two Canadian pilots from RAF squadrons as flight commanders formed the nucleus of the unit. Other pilots began arriving a few days later, most of them fresh out of training schools. (The RAF was reluctant to part with its experienced Canadian flyers and, besides, it wanted to minimize the disruption of other squadrons.) By the end of the month, 242 Squadron had its full complement of twenty-one pilots which included Slim Grassick, Marvin Brown, Willie McKnight and Stan Turner who, a month earlier, had crashed into a tree while night-flying in a Mentor.

Flight training now took place with three Magisters, one Harvard, and a Fairey Battle. On a visit to the station, the Group Air Officer Com-manding asked the pilots what operational aircraft they would prefer. To a man the answer was an enthusiastic "Spitfires!" In December, when seven Blenheim twin-engine fighters and three Battles arrived at Church Fenton, the dismay was equally unanimous. However, later in the month, the squadron received the welcome news it was to be refitted with Hur-ricanes.

Familiarization with the new fighters was hampered by one of the worst English winters on record and the biggest snowfall in forty years. It was not until March 1940 that the squadron was declared operational and began conducting convoy patrols off the east coast. During this period the pilots were the first to have "Canada" badges sewn onto the shoulders of their tunics, which became emblematic of overseas service. On April 1, word reached the squadron that it was to begin moving to France in ten days. Then, on April 8, the Germans invaded Denmark and the advance party which had been headed up by Noel Stansfeld, a former stockbroker from Vancouver, was recalled. For 242, it was now a case of wait and see.

# CHAPTER FIVE

# PRELUDE

On September 10, 1939, the day Canada declared war on Germany, No. 1 (Fighter) Squadron RCAF, now stationed at St. Hubert, P.Q., received orders from National Defence Headquarters in Ottawa to mobilize. Next day, although the ground crews and the crated Hurricanes were still enroute from Calgary, the squadron was placed on a wartime footing.

Ten days later, Ernie McNab took the train to Toronto to pick up a Hurricane that had been used as a static display at the Canadian National Exhibition which closed on Labour Day. By the third week of September, the pilots were flying again. On the 22nd, Ed Reyno conducted oxygen tests at 16,000 feet. At the beginning of November, McNab took over as CO and, two days later, the seven Hurricanes were flown to Dartmouth via Rimouski with an overnight stop at Moncton. The unit was now ready to become operational and was assigned coastal sweeps, naval escort duty, and practice exercises with army batteries and naval anti-aircraft guns.

On November 29, Ed Reyno carried out diving attacks on warships in the Bedford Basin to provide the anti-aircraft gunners with simulated defence experience. That same day, the squadron suffered its first casualty when one of the pilots crashed and was killed.

In May 1940, the squadron was amalgamated with 115 Auxiliary Squadron from Montreal whose pilots had been mobilized the day war was declared to begin training (by this time they all had their wings), and was further augmented with pilots from 8, 10 and 11 Bomber Reconnaissance Squadrons based in the Maritimes. The squadron was now up to full strength — and just in time.

In Europe, the Phoney War had ended on May 10 when the Wehrmacht, under heavy Luftwaffe cover, began its Blitzkrieg on the West, simultaneously striking at Holland, Belgium, Luxembourg and France. Twelve days later, No. 1 Squadron RCAF received orders to proceed overseas.

The Hurricanes were once again crated for shipment and the personnel innoculated. Meanwhile, in England, their Canadian cousins in 242 Squadron were thrown into a state of flux.

At first the unit was ordered to France, then on May 13 this order was countermanded. Half the pilots were to fly to the Continent to beef up RAF units which had already sustained losses in heavy fighting during the early days of the war. On the next day, Slim Grassick, Willie McKnight, Stan Turner and their flight commander arrived in France at Vitry-en-Artois to join 607 Squadron. That morning, on a patrol over Belgium near Louvain, the unit engaged forty-five Messerschmitt 109s escorting a group of Henschel 126 reconnaissance planes. Ten of the 109s were shot down but so were four Hurricanes, including the one flown by the 242 flight commander, who was killed.

Having made several more patrols over the next few days, Grassick and McKnight were transferred to 615 Squadron at Moorselle in Belgium. Next day, McKnight became the second Canadian in World War II to bring down an enemy plane when he scored against a Messerschmitt over Cambrai. At 7:04 a.m., seven of the German fighters dived on his patrol from 10,000 feet followed by eight more. McKnight spotted them first, called a warning over the R/T, then broke sharply to port. Approaching one of the 109s from behind, he opened fire from 250 yards with four short bursts, sending the German fighter crashing to the ground. On the 19th, McKnight nearly bought it himself. While strafing an enemy armoured column along the Arras-Cambrai Road, his fuel tanks were punctured by ground-fire.

Meanwhile, on May 16, Marvin Brown was among those members of "A" Flight that flew to France to join 85 Squadron at Lille. There on Saturday, May 18, in a patrol over Cateau, he and two others were shot down in a furious fight with a gaggle of Messerschmitt 110 twin-engine fighters. Wounded in the right leg, he was taken to an aid station then put in an ambulance heading for Cambrai. But, when the driver learned the Germans had captured the textile town, he drove to the coast where Brown was evacuated and hospitalized in England.

By May 20, most of the RAF squadrons in France had been withdrawn and 242 Squadron's pilots were making their various ways back to England. The rest of the squadron, which had moved to Biggin Hill in Kent, became part of the home-based fighter squadron assigned to fly patrols over France. On May 22, on a patrol between Doulens and Hesdin, Noel Stansfeld shared in the destruction of a Henschel reconnaissance aircraft. His combat report was terse and to the point: "I sighted enemy aircraft approaching cloud. I opened fire from the rear which apparently silenced the rear gunner. . . . The enemy aircraft stalled and headed for the ground nose down. It crashed and burst into flames."

Next day, John Benzie, a former member of the Princess Patricia's Canadian Light Infantry from Winnipeg, who joined 242 with Stansfeld, was wounded over Ypres when his flight was bounced by eighteen Me 109s. However, he managed to parachute to safety and was evacuated to England via Dunkirk. Others in his section were not so lucky. One pilot was killed and another, although able to bail out, fell into enemy hands and was taken prisoner.

The pilots who returned from France were granted seven days' leave. Within forty-eight hours it was cancelled, and the unit began operating from Manston on the southeast coast. By the evening of May 28, Operation Dynamo, the evacuation of the British army from Dunkirk, got underway. Two days later, Stan Turner scored his first victory. When an Me 109 dove on him over Ostend, Turner twisted and turned until he got on the enemy's tail. Then, from 150 yards, he delivered two three-second bursts that sent the German fighter down in flames.

Willie McKnight scored his second victory that day. He was firing at an Me 109 which turned away from him, when suddenly its engine stopped and the German fighter plunged headlong into the sea. But another 109 came in from the port beam and disabled the Hurricane's oil and coolant system. McKnight ducked into the clouds to escape with several other Messerschmitts on his tail. He reached Manston after what he described as "a determined and sustained chase by the enemy."

May 29 was a heyday for the Canadians. Attacking a Messerschmitt that had manoeuvred onto the tail of a Hurricane, Turner fired a short, sharp burst that sent the enemy fighter spinning down, smoking. Then a 109 got behind him. Pulling into a tight turn, he was soon in a position to open fire and the enemy fighter went down vertically.

McKnight was about to attack a Messerschmitt when the Hurricane he was flying with found another 109 on his tail. McKnight turned sharp right and opened fire at point-blank range. The enemy plane rolled onto its side and plunged into the sea. Turning away, McKnight attacked an Me 109 chasing a Hurricane. After a short burst of fire it began smoking and dove steeply for the shore. He then sighted a Dornier 17 twin-engine bomber above and to his right. He climbed at a steep angle and opened fire from the port rear-quarter. His first burst disabled the port engine and, with a last burst, it began smoking and crashed just east of Dunkirk.

Leading a section of three aircraft, Slim Grassick fired two bursts at a Messerschmitt which had dived below him and sent it down into the

Channel. He then attacked another enemy fighter which he damaged but, having spent all his ammunition, was unable to follow it down.

John Latta also accounted for an Me 109 destroyed. "I made my attack from dead astern," he later reported, "and after a burst of twelve seconds smoke poured out of the engine and the machine went into a dive." During the combat Latta's Hurricane was hit and he had to land at Manston on one wheel.

It had been a spectacular outing for Canada — five German aircraft destroyed, three probably destroyed, and two damaged without a single loss to the squadron. That night, Willie McKnight was awarded an immediate Distinguished Flying Cross, the first Canadian fighter pilot to be decorated in WWII. The citation to the award credited him with showing "exceptional skill and courage as a fighter pilot." And the Canadians were not quite through with Operation Dynamo. Two days later, while attacking an Me 110 bomber escort, Stansfeld destroyed one of the twin-engine fighters. McKnight, who joined the fray, accounted for two others when they collided just as he opened fire on them. Later, Latta brought down an Me 109 and Turner sent another plunging into the sea. Grassick rounded out the day's effort by destroying one more Messerschmitt.

On June 1, which saw the heaviest fighting of the Dunkirk evacuation, McKnight and Stansfeld dove into the middle of fifteen Junkers 87 Stuka dive-bombers. McKnight scored two confirmed victories and two probables, while Stansfeld was credited with one probable. Meanwhile, Turner shot down one Me 109 and probably destroyed another in the squadron's last action during Dynamo which ended on June 4. By then, 338,228 British and French troops had been successfully taken off the beaches.

For the RAF pilots, it had been a strangely detached experience. From above they could see the lines of soldiers packed so closely together that they somehow resembled swarms of ants. Chaos was everywhere — the burning oil tanks and wrecked vehicles. Boats of all sizes — warships, barges and even the Thames ferries — sailed back and forth, a ragtag armada. But it was all remote and distant, like watching a newsreel. Yet there existed an empathy on the part of the airmen for the lot of those on the ground. This was not a sentiment reciprocated by the army or, for that matter, the navy. The men on the beaches were unaware of the epic being fought out above them. Most of the combat occurred often miles away or above the clouds, and what aircraft they did see they could not identify as friend or foe. Bombed unmercifully, they expected protection. Here, with the German assault only three weeks old, they were being bundled out of France and they resented it. They felt that if the air force had done its job they could have held the line. And always the bombing continued. They had no idea how much of it the RAF had prevented.

In fact, the might and power of the Luftwaffe had been blooded for the first time even though the RAF was not only badly outnumbered but beyond radar range. The pilots had to fly by ear, relying on their own visual powers to find the enemy. Yet in only nine days they had nevertheless destroyed 377 German planes against a loss of only eighty-seven of their own. In the case of 242 Squadron, those losses had reached serious proportions and threatened the unit's Canadian identity. Since May 14, the pilots had shot down twenty-one enemy machines, probably destroyed seven, and damaged eight. But the Canadians had lost fifteen in killed, wounded and captured, and as there were few Canadians among the replacements, the RCAF authorities in Great Britain expressed some alarm. This was chauvinistic and a bit petty and was really of little consequence. What counted most was to bring the squadron up to strength as quickly as possible. Where the battle on the Continent was concerned, there was still work to do. The French were still fighting, even though the German advance was unstoppable.

South of the Somme, Britain still had one army division in France which had been withdrawn earlier from the Maginot Line, and a second division which was landed at Normandy. These were now to be augmented with a reconstituted division from the forces evacuated at Dunkirk, which was landing at Le Havre, and the 1st Canadian Division which landed at Brest.

To support the remaining three fighter squadrons of the British Advanced Striking Force, on June 8, 242 Squadron along with another flew to Le Mans and then Châteaudun, northeast of Orleans and southwest of Paris. A field servicing crew was brought in by Harrow transport in relays, but they were unable to carry out extensive repairs. Any seriously damaged aircraft would have to be abandoned.

From there the squadron flew to a field to the north to carry out duties in the Le Havre area. These flights were a mixture of offensive patrols and bomber escort sorties. During the first of these on June 9, Stan Turner brought down an Me 109.

Almost simultaneously that same day, Johnny Kent had his first encounter with German fighters — in a slow 120-mile-per-hour Tiger Moth trainer! In France, the Photographic Development Unit had been reduced from three airfields to one at Meaux, forty miles east of Paris. But now, with the French army in disarray and the Germans advancing willy-nilly in any direction they chose, the unit was ordered to clear out and make for Bricy, south of Orleans. Kent and one other pilot were all that remained after the main party took off, and all they had were two Tiger Moths. Kent had just climbed into one machine when a German formation of twin-engine Junkers 88s started to drop bombs on the field from 8,000 feet.

Kent opened the throttle wide and took off. As he left the ground and made an immediate turn, the first bombs began bursting on the edge of the field. Petrified, he kept the tiny aircraft at tree-top level as did the other pilot, and luckily the German crews completely ignored them. An hour later, much relieved, they landed at their destination.

* * *

Although it was of little concern or consequence, and certainly of no consolation for the crude conditions under which the Canadians laboured in France, they might nevertheless have liked to know that at 10 a.m. on June 11, No. 1 Squadron RCAF and its crated Hurricanes had set sail from Halifax aboard the steamship Duchess of Atholl. Escorted by three destroyers and one battleship, a patrol of RCAF Stranraer aircraft accompanied the convoy until dusk.

By June 13, the German advance began to threaten Châteaudun and, over the next five days, 242 Squadron made a series of moves to the west. On the following day, however, when attacked by a dozen Me 109s over the Seine River near Paris, the squadron shot down all twelve of the enemy fighters, McKnight accounting for two of them.

At this point it was no longer possible to conduct high-altitude aerial reconnaissance. Haze and smoke from fires and burning oil tanks obscured visibility. The photographic missions now had to be carried out at low level. As a result, the Spitfires were re-equipped with eight Browning machine-guns. On his first flight in one of the rearmed aircraft, Kent got into a scrap with a flight of Me 109s.

Singling out one of them at 3,000 feet, he took aim when suddenly the German pilot made a half roll and went into a dive. Kent followed, then realizing he was coming too low to the ground too fast, he quickly broke off the attack and pulled up. Just in time; as he came out of the dive he was right down on the deck between two river embankments. The Me 109 pilot was not as lucky. His plane crashed into the ground, or so Kent surmised when, out of the corner of his eye, he suddenly saw a red flash and a plume of smoke.

By the night of June 15, orders were issued for the main body of 242 Squadron's ground crew to sail for England via St. Nazaire on the west coast of Brittany at the mouth of the Loire River, leaving a small rearguard party behind. Now the pilots had to help refuel, service and repair their aircraft themselves. The British army had begun to evacuate, first through Le Havre and, when that port was overrun, from St. Nazaire. Neil Campbell of St. Thomas, one of 242's pilots, wrote home: "We covered the evacuation from Nantes and prevented it from becoming another Dunkirk."

The British troops made their escape on the afternoon of June 18. After flying a final patrol on June 19, 242's pilots, battered and tired, took off on what constituted an endurance test for the Hurricane — a two-and-a-half-hour flight to Tangmere. After refueling they continued on to Coltishall in Norfolk, north of Norwich. Meanwhile, the ground crew rearguard set fire to all equipment and unserviceable aircraft and then boarded the Harrow for England. Several hours later, German Panzers came rumbling over the cobblestones into Nantes.

# CHAPTER SIX

# BREATHER

All that stood in the way of a German invasion of Great Britain were the remains of the British army and the RAF. The surrender of the country depended upon whether the RAF could prevent the Luftwaffe from wiping out or grounding its fighter squadrons. Without them, the Royal Navy could never survive if the Germans gained control of the air.

After the fall of France, the RAF had been reduced to 331 Spitfires and Hurricanes. The good news was that on May 14, Winston Churchill, who had taken over as prime minister, placed the Ministry of Aircraft Production in the hands of the energetic Canadian newspaper tycoon, Lord Beaverbrook. The bad news was that the force had been so depleted by losses in France and at Dunkirk that there were only 360 fighter pilots, well short of the complement of 1,450. Mackenzie King's refusal to cooperate in the Empire Training Scheme in 1937 had begun to hurt. Though one extra squadron represented a mere drop in the fuel tank, the arrival of No. 1 Fighter Squadron RCAF at Liverpool on June 20, two days before the French surrender, was at least a flight in the right direction.

Next day, the unit entrained for Middle Wallop. Because the station was under construction, some personnel were housed in tents while others were billeted out in the village. When the commander-in-chief of RAF Fighter Command, Hugh "Stuffy" Dowding, learned on a visit to the squadron several days later that the Hurricanes being uncrated and reassembled were not the latest type, he promptly made arrangements to have them replaced by new ones. Beaverbrook's dynamism was already beginning to pay off. In February, the factories had turned out 140 fighters. Under the Beaver's direction, in May this had been boosted to 325 and, by the end of June, the monthly output would be 446 with the promise of an even higher quota the following month.

Meanwhile, on June 27, Gordie McGregor and Charles Briese carried out test flights on two Harvards to get their hands back in. Though the Battle of Britain was yet to begin, the squadron, based at Coltishall, experienced its first air raid the following night when a stick of bombs was dropped on the station.

By this time, to the north, Douglas Bader, the famous legless pilot, had taken over command of 242 Squadron. He found the pilots a discouraged, dishevelled lot who did not even stand up when he entered the dispersal hut. A Cranwell College graduate, in his best, most military manner, he proceeded to tear a strip off them for their appearance, their attitude, their lack of discipline. This earned a curt rebuke from Stan Turner who retorted "Bullshit!", then punctuated it with a half-hearted, semi-respectful "Sir."

When the airmen explained what they had been through during the final stages of the Battle of France, Bader grudgingly apologized and embarked on a program of reorganization. He also worked to boost moral. Replacements arrived, the first two in the form of flight commanders, and both were British. Also among the new arrivals were two Canadians: George Christie, who had flown with the Photographic Development Unit in France, and Norrie Hart from Montreal.

Because, except for their aircraft, the squadron had left even the most basic tools behind in the retreat from the Continent, new tools along with spare parts and servicing equipment had to be acquired. It took some days before these arrived, and then the squadron settled into a period of intense training. This was pretty well the case with all the other squadrons that had escaped from France.

No. 1 RAF Squadron, of which Hilly Brown had been made a flight commander, had only ten Hurricanes and eleven pilots left when it arrived back at Tangmere. Brown had been shot down on the way home and had to hitch a ride aboard the last troopship leaving Brest. Though the squadron was declared operational, on July 3 it was judged unfit for combat and ordered to temporarily limit its activity to training and testing flights.

Next day, No. 1 Squadron RCAF left Middle Wallop to begin combat exercises at Croyden aerodrome.

At noon on July 9, 242 Squadron was declared operational. And despite Bader's earlier misgivings, he was happy with his pilots — particularly the Canadians. He rated Willie McKnight and Stan Turner as two of the best he'd ever seen. He wasn't too upset, either, when Noel Stansfeld got the highest number of hits during an air-firing exercise in which the squadron posted a scoring record for Fighter Command.

On the morning of July 10, his revitalized squadron drew first blood on a convoy patrol off the Norfolk coast. One of the pilots shot down a Heinkel 111 that was attempting to bomb the ships, while John Latta damaged another. The bomber escaped into a cloud at 4,000 feet, its starboard engine smoking. But it still made Latta the first Canadian to chalk up a score in the Battle of Britain, then only scant hours old.

# CHAPTER SEVEN

# OPENING PHASE

Between the end of the Battle of France and the start of the Battle of Britain, Dowding had been given a breathing spell in which to marshal his forces. By July, his Order of Battle showed fifty-two fighter squadrons, of which twenty-two had Hurricanes and nineteen had Spitfires. Seven were equipped with slow, twin-engine Blenheims, and two had Boulton Paul Defiants.

The Defiant was a single-engine, two-seater aircraft that looked somewhat like the Hurricane from a distance, and it enjoyed a brief moment of surprising success at Dunkirk. But the Me 109 pilots soon got wise to the four-gun rear-turret and attacked the Defiant from the front where the aircraft had no armament, or from below and underneath where its guns could not be brought to bear. Duke Arthur of Fort Garry, Man., and Arthur Smith of Summerland, B.C., flying with 141 Squadron from West Malling, would shortly be lucky to survive a battle in which their formation was cut to ribbons by Messerschmitt astern attacks.

In terms of numbers, 528 single-seater fighters stood ready to meet the German air assault. Arrayed against them, the Luftwaffe forces seemed awesome. Two *Luftflottes* — Air Fleets — comprised of 1,800 aircraft, 1,000 of which were bombers, along with 650 Me 109 fighters, and 160 Me 110 fighters, faced the south of England.

Although badly outnumbered, the RAF nonetheless had several things going for it. Its early warning system made up of fifty radar stations meant that enemy formations could be detected before they reached the coast, and the British aircraft could be vectored onto them before they got to their targets. The Germans knew that the RAF had radar, but had no idea what impact it had on British defences. It came as a grim shock when their pilots found British fighters waiting for them over England.

In the southern half of the British Isles, Fighter Command was divided into three sectors which gave it maximum flexibility in battle. Sixteen squadrons made up 11 Group that guarded the approaches to London from Portsmouth to the Thames Estuary. It represented a force of 195 aircraft upon whom the bulk of the fighting would fall.

The east coast and the Midlands were defended by 12 Group, comprised of eleven single-seater squadrons to protect the north and northeast of England with its 120 aircraft. A third group, No. 10, was responsible for the area in the south from Portsmouth westward.

Finally, the discovery of Enigma (from the Greek "puzzle"), the code-breaking apparatus that intercepted all messages from the German High Command, meant the British had advanced information about the Luftwaffe's plans. Enigma also provided access to directives from Adolf Hitler and Hermann Goering. All this enabled Dowding to plot his strategy.

The delay in getting the air attack underway after the fall of France had, ironically, been Hitler's. The German Fuehrer had been confident that, faced with an air assault, and possibly an invasion, Britain would prefer to settle with Germany. His "Last Appeal to Reason" proclamation by pamphlet had already been laughed off by John Bulldog. He was now preparing to make a proper peace proposal to England in a speech to the Reichstag when, on July 4, the Royal Navy attacked French battleships at Oran harbour in North Africa to prevent them falling into German hands. Three days later, Hitler had decided to "unleash a storm of fire and steel on the British."

As plans for Operation Sea Lion, the invasion of Britain, got underway, Erich Raeder, Commander of the German *Kriegsmarine*, announced that he was opposed to the operation. He wanted to implement a naval blockade instead to starve the island into surrender. Nevertheless, he agreed that if it was going to take place, "Command of the air is a necessary condition."

Goering and his Luftwaffe chief of the Air Staff, Hans Jeschonnek, were confident after the experience in the Polish and French campaigns that an aerial assault on England would be nothing more than a fly-past. Occupation by the German army would be a mere formality, at best a quick *coup d'état*.

Alfred Jodl, chief of the staff to the head of the *Oberkommando Wehrmacht* — OKW (Military High Command) — was just as sure of the outcome. He calculated that after the RAF had been sent reeling by the Luftwaffe, the same treatment could be extended to Britain's food and supplies, with occasional "terror attacks" on the civilian population.

This, he was sure, "would break the will of the people to resist and force their government to capitulate." He forecast an English surrender by August, or at the very latest in early September.

The first objective of the Battle of Britain was to clear the Channel of shipping. Dowding had not counted on having to provide protection for convoys and knew that the Germans were trying to lure his fighters out to sea in what could become a battle of attrition if he failed to husband his resources. The *Kanalkampf* — Channel battle — was a win-lose proposition. If Dowding refused to commit his fighters, British ships would be sunk. In addition, the radar was not all that effective at this stage. The German aircraft could form up and reach heights out of its range. Then, once they were detected, it would take British fighters at least fifteen minutes to climb to altitude. For these reasons, Dowding's protection of the convoys was therefore limited to small formations. Even at that, by the end of July Fighter Command had lost 118 aircraft. It was small consolation that Luftwaffe losses of 190 were some sixty percent higher.

On July 12, flying a Spitfire from St. Eval with 234 Squadron, Ken Lawrence of Halifax who, four days earlier, had shared in shooting down a Junkers 88 bomber, was credited with probably destroying another 88. On that same date, Canada suffered its first casualty of the battle when Duncan "Alex" Hewitt of St. John, N.B., a Hurricane pilot with 501 Squadron at Middle Wallop, was killed in action.

The worst day of that month for the RAF was July 19. This was the date the Boulton Paul Defiants were sent into the battle for the first — and last — time. It was a total wipe. In the early afternoon, nine of the two-seater aircraft from 141 Squadron took off from Hawkinge on the south coast, three Canadians among them: Duke Arthur, Arthur Smith and Alex Howley of Victoria, B.C.

As soon as they were airborne, they were ordered to patrol south of Folkestone at 5,000 feet. At 1:00 p.m., Messerschmitt 109s led by Hannes Trautloft of 3rd Gruppe, Jagdstaffel 51, escorted Walter Rubensdorffer's Erp Gruppe 210 Me 110 fighter-bombers on a raid against a British trawler which they quickly sunk. Having escorted the 110s back to France, Trautloft, a veteran of the Spanish Civil War, decided to lead his Gruppe back over the Channel in search of RAF fighters. At 1:43 one of his pilots spotted a British formation. As they got closer they could see the rear gun-turrets which clearly identified them as Defiants.

Attacking out of the sun, Trautloft led his Me 109s down astern and below the two-seater fighters. The bounce was quick, sharp and deadly. "Most of us were hit within seconds and six were going down," Arthur later recalled. Howley was killed instantly. Arthur's Defiant and that of Smith would also have been knocked out had it not been for the intervention of Hurricanes from 111 Squadron which came to the rescue. In chasing the German fighters off, they shot down one Me 109 and damaged Trautloft's machine so badly he was forced to crash-land at St. Inglevert, just in from the French coast.

One of the Defiants that had been hit managed to make it back to Hawkinge where it crashed on landing, but when the pilot turned around he discovered the rear cockpit was empty. The body of his air-gunner was never found. In all, four pilots and six air-gunners from 141 Squadron were killed in a matter of seconds. It was a completely shattered squadron that evening at Hawkinge. What was left of it was moved north to Prestwick in Scotland where the Defiants were assigned night-fighter duties.

Off-setting the Defiant fiasco that day was the small redeeming feature that Camille Bonseigneur from Regina became the third Canadian to score in the battle. Flying a Hurricane with 17 Squadron, he shared in the destruction of a Dornier 17 twin-engine bomber.

And where Canada was concerned, for the rest of the month there was more good news. On July 20, Lionel Gaunce, in a Hurricane, shot down a Messerschmitt 109. Four days later, Johnny Bryson, a burly ex-Mountie from Montreal, now a Spitfire pilot with 92 Squadron, shared in shooting down a Ju 88. On the following day Ray Wilson, from Moncton, based at Croyden, destroyed one Me 109 and damaged another. On July 30, Harry "Hammy" Hamilton from Oak Point, N.B, flying a Hurricane with 85 Squadron from Martlesham Heath, brought down a twin-engine Me 110.

July had been largely a period of experiment. A month of give and take, thrust and parry, feint and lunge, fancy flywork on both sides. A cautious test of will and strength in which the principal antagonists of the battle, Dowding and Goering, sparred warily. David saving his slingshot while Goliath champed at the bit. Then, on August 1, an impatient Hitler broke that cross-Channel stand-off with his Fuehrer Directive No. 17. It pulled no punches. "I intend to intensify air and sea warfare against the English homeland," he declared. Explicitly he ordered that: "The Luftwaffe is to overpower the Royal Air Force . . . in the shortest possible time." Early that morning two Canadian fighter pilots had done their level best to deny him that directive.

# CHAPTER EIGHT

# ADLERANGRIFF

At 5:47 a.m., George Christie, John Latta and another colleague took off from Coltishall to protect a convoy making its way south off Lowestoft. A solid layer of overcast hovered between 1,000 and 2,000 feet, and by the time they reached the ships they were already under sporadic attack from Junkers 88s and Heinkel 111s. Because of the haze and resulting impaired visibility, their bombs fell well wide of the mark.

Latta took potshots at three different bombers while Christie fired at another. Neither of them had any luck and they returned to guard the convoy. Then, just before seven o'clock, the Germans attacked again. Christie singled out a Junkers and chased it into the clouds but was forced to break off when he ran out of ammunition. He was credited with the probable destruction of the bomber when, in fact, he had so badly damaged the aircraft, which belonged to 2nd Gruppe Kampfgeschwader 30, that it crash-landed in Denmark. In the mêlée, two of the crew were killed and a third wounded.

Coltishall, located as it was in 12 Group, was well out of the main battle area. When the German attacks later intensified, its squadrons would operate from Duxford further south to take part in the main action. That move was to have turbulent ramifications not only during the battle but also in its aftermath. For the moment, however, the units had to content themselves with convoy patrols.

About this time Johnny Kent had been posted to Northolt as a flight commander of a new squadron, No. 303, being formed with Polish pilots who had escaped from their country when the Germans overran it. They were a very keen bunch but had two serious drawbacks. First, they were unfamiliar with retractable undercarriages which led to a rash of wheels-up landings. Second, they spoke no English. (There was one exception; their engineering officer had mastered a phrase, but only one: "Come on boys!") Kent had his work cut out for him, not only training them to fly Hurricanes but also teaching them English.

Ernie McNab had insisted that his pilots be put through a period of combat training before being sent into battle. However, in his own case he abandoned his precept and requested transfer to an operational unit to get fighting experience at first hand. He and Flight Commander Gordie McGregor were promptly attached on a temporary basis to 111 Squadron, a Hurricane outfit stationed at Croyden.

Meanwhile, Canadian presence was being felt in no uncertain terms throughout the RAF elsewhere. By August 8, Andrew Fletcher, a Blenheim pilot from Cardston, Alta., had scored against two German planes; he shot down an Me 110 and damaged a Heinkel 115 seaplane. That same day, Arthur "Jimmy" Cochrane of Vernon, B.C., flying with 257 Squadron out of Tangmere, in his very first combat, clobbered an Me 109 while on convoy duty off St. Catherine's Point.

On August 11, Canadians accounted for three German aircraft destroyed and two damaged. Bill Nelson, who had won the Distinguished Flying Cross flying twin-engine Whitley bombers before joining 74 Squadron at Hornchurch, downed an Me 109, an Me 110, and damaged another of the twin-engine fighters. Hilly Brown also destroyed a 110, his first score in the battle. John "Pete" Gordon from Red Deer, Alta., a member of 615 Squadron, scored as well, damaging a Junkers 87 Stuka dive-bomber. Significantly, Ernie McNab brought down a Dornier 17 bomber that day to become the second RCAF pilot to score a victory in the air. On the obverse side, Robert "Ray" Wilson of Moncton, N.B. became Canada's third casualty of the battle. A Hurricane pilot with 111 Squadron, he was killed while attacking a section of Dornier 215s.

That morning, Me 110s had bombed Dover harbour at first light. But Keith Park, commander of 11 Group, refused at first to allow his fighters to be sucked in while waiting for the bombers to make their move. As the morning wore on, however, more and more squadrons were scrambled and a succession of engagements took place. At ten o'clock, as 165 German bombers, heavily escorted by Me 109s and 110s, reached mid-Channel, eight RAF fighter squadrons were sent to meet them. They were soon embroiled in bitter and costly fighting with the German fighters while the Luftwaffe bombers were allowed to attack Portland and Weymouth almost unscathed. That afternoon saw more heavy fighting as each side sought to rescue downed flyers from the sea. During the day's fighting, the British shot down thirty-five aircraft against a loss of thirty of their own.

This was the last day of the *Kanalkampf*, a prelude to the Wagnerian sounding *Adlerangriff* — the Eagle Attack — massive assaults against British airfields and RAF fighters, which Goering now believed could be wiped out in four days. Scheduled to begin on August 6, it had been postponed to start on August 12 with *Adlertag* — Eagle Day — set for the following day.

Monday, August 12, dawned bright and clear, a perfect summer's day, ideal for Luftwaffe bomber attacks on Britain's airfields and radar stations. Manston aerodrome on the east coast took a fearful pounding and the Ventnor radar station was knocked out although the Germans didn't know it. The RAF lost thirty fighters but in turn destroyed thirty-one German aircraft. Two Canadians contributed to the British score. Jimmy Cochrane destroyed a Messerschmitt 109 and damaged a Heinkel 111. Lionel Gaunce, now a flight commander with 615 Squadron, posted his third victory by destroying a 109. That same day another Hurricane pilot, Robert Beley of Rossland, B.C. with 151 Squadron, became the first Canadian to die of wounds sustained in aerial combat.

On Tuesday, Goering cancelled Eagle Day for the moment, but Johannes "Papa" Fink's Kampfgeschwader 2 headquarters at Arras, France, never received the order. So Fink took off at the head of seventy Dornier 17s from his Geschwader across the Channel. However, his Me 110 escort had answered the recall and turned back after futilely trying to signal Fink to abort, with the result the Dorniers were on their own with no fighter escort.

Fink's aircrews bombed the airfields at Eastchurch and Sheerness with lethal accuracy, but one Gruppe was badly mauled by Spitfires. Heavy losses for both sides continued: twenty for the RAF, twenty-seven for the Luftwaffe. Three pilots won victories for Canada. Joe Laricheliere, flying a Hurricane from Exeter with 213 Squadron, performed a hat-trick when he shot down a Junkers 88, a Messerschmitt 109 and a 110 in quick succession. Bill Nelson, the former bomber pilot, nailed two Dorniers, a 17 and a 215, while Bill Fiske of 601 Squadron brought his Hurricane's sights to bear on a Ju 88 which he put away in short order. Four days later he died of wounds received in a dogfight, the second such Canadian casualty in the battle.

August 14 was a day of light skirmishes which allowed Dowding to retire three of his most battered squadrons to a quieter sector to rest up. Nonetheless, on that date Harold Mitchell from Mount Hope, Ont., shot down a Ju 87 Stuka and also destroyed one Me 110 and damaged another. Pete Gordon, who a week earlier had been made CO of 151 Squadron, also got into the act, shooting down an Me 109.

Eagle Day, April 15, proved to be a debacle for the Luftwaffe. It lost between fifty-five and seventy-five planes, the highest casualty figure of the entire battle. The Norwegian and Denmark-based Luftflotte 5, which raided the north of England, was virtually wiped out. Hiram Smith from Edmonton, flight commander with 72 Squadron flying out of Acklington, joined in the shoot-out by destroying one Ju 88 and damaging another with his Spitfire. That airfleet never returned to the battle.

Other Canadians figuring in the duel for the sky to the south were Butch Barton who damaged one 110 and destroyed another; and Joe Laricheliere who scored his second hat-trick by destroying a Ju 87 and two Me 110s. That was his last fight, however. He was killed next day.

Total losses for the day were twenty-eight fighters. This included a Canadian casualty, James "Swede" Johnston from Brandon, Man. Like Robert Beley, who died from wounds three days earlier, Johnston also flew Hurricanes with 151 Squadron out of North Weald.

Hilly Brown was luckier. When his Hurricane caught fire he was forced to ditch in the sea off Felixstowe and was picked up by a trawler. He suffered a minor leg injury that only kept him out of the fighting for a few days.

Significantly, only eight Me 109s were shot down. The single-engine Luftwaffe pilots were holding their own. But the British policy of concentrating on the bombers had made a large dent in that force. And these losses did not take into account the numbers of dead and wounded aboard the returning aircraft.

The Germans marked the day *Der Schwartz Donnerstag* — Black Thursday. And it was made even blacker by an edict delivered at a conference held that day at Goering's sumptuous headquarters at Karinhall. Officer-aircrew casualties had become so severe that the *Reichsmarschall* decreed that not more than one officer would be allowed to fly in each aircraft, and that Stuka dive-bombers must have no less than three fighters each for protection. Then, in one of the greatest blunders not only of the Battle of Britain but of the entire war, he added: "It is doubtful whether there is any point in continuing the attacks on radar stations, in view of the fact that not one of those attacked so far has been put out of action."

# CHAPTER NINE

# THE LULL

On the day after *Adlertag*, No. 1 Fighter Squadron RCAF, which had been undergoing training at Croydon, got ready to move to Northolt. There it would soon take part in the real thing.

Despite Goering's order, that afternoon by accident during a German raid on airfields in the south of England, the Ventnor radar station was put out of action, this time for a week. If the *Reichsmarschall* had only known how badly this gap had blinded the British seeing-eye defence system. But at this point his air force had its own concerns.

The last two days of hectic fighting had taken a toll on the German aircrew. The Luftwaffe needed a break to catch its breath. Further operations for Airfleets 2 and 3 were put on hold to give the weary airmen a rest and for crews to repair damaged aircraft as well as to replace men and machines.

Keith Park, 11 Group commander, had decided that instead of concentrating on the German bombers he would send the Spitfires to engage the high-flying fighter escorts while the Hurricanes waded into the bomber formations. This was provisional; shooting down the marauders still remained the top priority.

The Germans had opted for a change of tactics as well. They decided that their fighters should now fly close-escort to the bombers. It would give the bomber crews a lift to see their own fighters buzzing around them, protecting their flock. But that was a moot point. To stay with them, the Messerschmitt 109s would have to slow their pace to that of the bombers.

August 17 saw a brief respite from the fighting. By this time, four new Canadian faces had appeared on Bader's 242 Squadron roster at Coltishall. These were Hugh Tamblyn from Watrous, Sask.; John Cave of Calgary who had served with 600 Squadron; Laurie Cryderman, a former Toronto school-teacher and a whiz on the piano; and Kirkpatrick

Sclanders from Saskatoon, Sask., who first flew when he was fifteen years old.

Goering was now hard-pressed to destroy Fighter Command if Hitler's schedule to launch twenty-five army divisions against England between Folkestone and Worthington by September 21 was to be maintained. As a consequence, severe air fighting erupted over Great Britain again on August 18. It was Eagle Day all over again, a final flourish by Goering to knock out RAF fighter fields. Biggin Hill, Croyden, Kenley, Manston and West Malling aerodromes were hit hard by low-level raids. But the toll on German aircrew toll was again horrendous; seventy-one aircraft were lost. RAF casualties amounted to twenty-seven fighters with ten pilots killed. However, the difference between the British and German losses was not only in ratios. If an RAF pilot crash-landed or bailed out safely, he could fight another day. In fact, Park was about to instruct his controllers not to vector any more of his fighters over the Channel, but only overland where they could parachute, glide down or force-land. Had this been implemented sooner, a lot of grief would have been spared No. 1 Fighter Squadron RCAF. For the Germans it was a different story. Planes shot down over England resulted in captured aircrew and aircraft.

The losses that day told another tale. In the raid on Kenley alone, ten Junkers 88s and Dornier 17s from Kampfgeschwader 76 had been shot down. As a result, Goering banned any further low-level attacks. In a stroke he had eliminated one of the menaces the RAF feared most.

That day also knelled the death of the Stuka. Sixteen of the dive-bombers had been shot down. Goering realized at last what easy targets they made and withdrew them from any further participation in the battle.

Three Canadians looked at the day's operations quite differently. Both Jimmy Cochrane and "Hammy" Hamilton were in high spirits, each having scored twice in the day's fighting. It brought Hamilton's list of victories to three. Nor was "Corporal" Lionel Gaunce disappointed when he damaged an Me 110, giving him a total of three destroyed, one probable and one damaged.

At Northolt, a reunion took place between two old friends, Johnny Kent and Ernie McNab, dating back to 1931. No. 1 Fighter Squadron RCAF's arrival, complementing Kent's 303 Polish Squadron and No. 1 RAF Squadron, made the station a truly cosmopolitan one. Both Kent's and McNab's units looked with envy on the British squadron which been getting a large share of the action lately. But their turn was soon to come, though for the moment they would have to wait.

Desultory weather set in for the next five days as if the curtain had come down signalling an intermission. Aircrews, ground crews, controllers

— just about anyone involved in the battle on both sides — needed the break. One Canadian pilot managed to use the recess to advantage, however, even though he was stationed in the "quiet" 12 Group sector to the north. On August 21, John Latta of 242 Squadron added to his tally when he shared in the destruction of a Dornier with two others.

Two days later, Lionel Gaunce was awarded the DFC "for his coolness and leadership . . . " The next day the weather cleared and the Battle of Britain entered its most crucial phase.

## CHAPTER TEN

# TRIAL AND ERROR

For his new offensive to obliterate Fighter Command within a week, Goering picked the ring of airfields just south of London as his prime target, to be bombed in daylight. This stretched the Me 109's range to the limit — a round trip of 390 miles — so that most of the German fighter *Staffels*, the equivalent of British squadrons, had been moved to the Pas de Calais, twenty miles across the Channel from the English coast. At night the bombers were to concentrate on industrial centres, some well beyond the British capital and to the west. The purpose was to slow production, particularly aircraft manufacturing.

Early on the cloudless morning of August 24, a large Luftwaffe formation of bombers and fighters began forming up over Cap Gris Nez. Earlier, pilots of 85 Squadron at Croydon were awakened by a bomb that exploded setting two Hurricanes on fire. It not only woke them up, but it got them out of bed. As they headed for the washrooms, the alarm sounded for a scramble and they had to abandon their ablutions and run for their Hurricanes.

After a brief skirmish with the 109 close-escorts, the pilots landed back at the field to find that the Duke of Kent had arrived on a visit and wanted to meet them. After dutifully lining up, Peter Townsend had just been presented when Hammy Hamilton let out a guffaw. Sticking out of the squadron CO's breast pocket, below his DFC ribbon and wings, was the toothbrush he'd forgotten to leave behind when the Klaxon horn sounded; he had taken it into battle with him. Even the Duke found it hard to suppress a regal grin. For Hamilton it was comic relief to a tragedy he learned of afterwards involving his fellow-countrymen late that afternoon.

At 3:57 p.m., twelve Hurricanes from No. 1 Fighter Squadron RCAF climbed to 10,000 feet to patrol the coast in the Tangmere area, their first time on operations (ops). The weather had turned somewhat misty, making it hard to see, but at 4:30 p.m. five aircraft were spotted 2,000 feet below flying north in line astern towards Portsmouth. In the interception that ensued, Ernie McNab and Paul Pitcher recognized the aircraft as Blenheims and broke away. However, Gordie McGregor and Paul Desloges attacked and claimed to have destroyed a Junkers 88. Deane Nesbitt, Arthur Yuile and Bill Sprenger reported strikes on another Ju 88. Lamentably, their targets turned out to be Blenheims from 235 Squadron RAF Coastal Command.

One of the British fighter-bombers was set on fire and plunged into the Channel where it sank with all three of its crew aboard. The other was luckier. Though it crash-landed on the aerodrome at Thorney Island, the crew were lucky to get away with a few cuts and bruises.

The entire affair, if unacceptable by any standards, was still a case of understandable mistaken identity. Even in the clearest visibility the Blenheim and the Junkers looked extremely alike in the air; silhouetted from any angle, particularly abeam or astern, both appeared similar. Each aircraft had twin-engines mounted in radial cowlings mid-wing vertically and laterally. The tail sections could have been virtually interchangeable. The fuselage as viewed from above was the same shape.

There was one signal difference between the two, although it was far from distinctive. The Blenheim had a rear gun-turret halfway along the top of the fuselage, but it was sunken so that from a hasty glance at a distance it was wellnigh unobtrusive. In his combat report, Sprenger stated: "The e/a [enemy aircraft] was low-winged, appeared to have radial engines, *had no gun turret on top side of fuselage* . . . "* The attacks in each case were made from the rear, and all the pilots maintained that the top of the fuselage appeared to be very dark, almost black. Most of them recorded that they did not see or identify any kind of markings to indicate the aircraft's origin.

But besides mistaken identity, other factors also entered the picture. Except for McNab, this was the first time these pilots had been sent out on an operational patrol. They were naturally nervous, probably over-eager. All the more so when some of them believed they were experiencing enemy return gunfire. Sprenger reported: "During my attack tracer bullets split past my windshield." Actually, these were red and yellow Very pistol flares fired by one of the Blenheims, the colours of the day signalling they were friendly. To add irony to the incident, on landing Paul Pitcher reported that when he had decided the aircraft were possibly British, he

---

*Emphasis is the author's.

BRISTOL BLENHEIM 1F

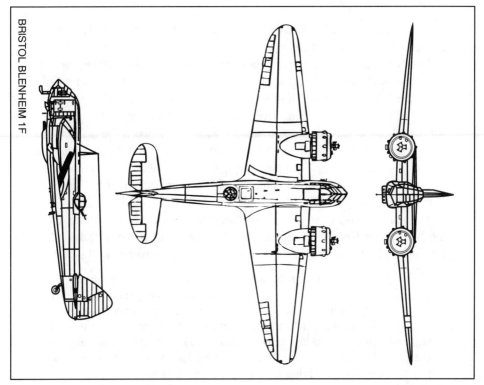

JUNKERS JU 88A-1

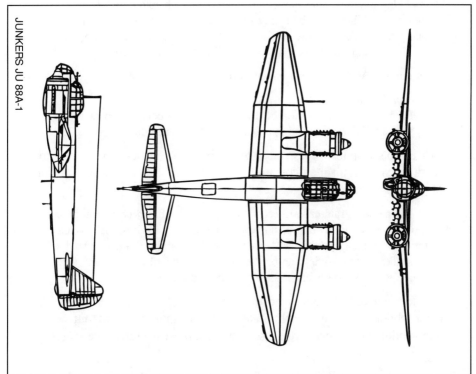

had radioed "Friendly Aircraft." But for some unexplained reason his transmission was never received.

This was not the first such incident. Only two days earlier, one of Johnny Kent's Polish pilots nearly shot down a Hurricane. Nor would it be the last. Graf von Moltke, the Prussian field marshal, said, "War is full of surprises." He could well have added "mistakes" also. But this was small consolation to the Canadians when they learned the truth about their action. Unofficially, Ernie McNab immediately visited 235 Squadron to pay his own and his unit's respects, offer apologies and condolences. These were accepted sympathetically, philosophically, all in the spirit of *c'est la guerre.*

The matter was not so easily dismissed officially. However, a letter from the Air Officer Commanding the RCAF overseas to Ernie McNab did illustrate the British Air Ministry's tendency to show leniency in the matter:

> The Air Ministry's view is that, while no purpose will be served by taking any severe disciplinary action against those responsible, the matter cannot simply be allowed to lapse without some formal notice being given of it. The Air Ministry naturally fully realize that this incident, while most regrettable, was entirely due to inexperience and excitement of No. 1 Squadron's [RCAF] first patrol; nevertheless, they laid a clear policy that the responsibility for identifying a friendly aircraft rests with the pilot of the attacking aircraft under any circumstances, and therefore in this instance the responsibility must be firmly fixed and brought home to the pilot or pilots concerned. The Air Ministry is entirely willing that any action taken in this respect is to be taken by the RCAF rather than the RAF.

Under the AOC's letter a handwritten addendum read:

> *Personal Note*
> There will be no question of disciplinary action being taken other than by the AOC himself — and in any event, nothing exceeding a rebuke.

McNab's response was typical of his brand of leadership, a deep and sensitive concern for the pilots under his command. After hearing a report of what had happened, he wrote:

> The mental strain experienced by the pilots . . . has been a punishment more severe than any that could be physically given, for it is not a pleasant thought to imagine one has been responsible for the death of two [sic] comrades. It was some time before these officers settled down and a repetition would seriously effect the efficiency of the unit.

The affair did not quite end there, however. The squadron operations record book that day simply stated that the unit was sent out on an interception but returned to base, having landed at Tangmere to refuel.

RCAF headquarters did not notify National Defence in Ottawa about the tragic ramifications until after the war, and then only in response to an official request. On February 27, 1947, it replied:

> The five combat reports submitted by No. 1 Canadian Squadron dated 24 August, 1940, and queried in your reference letter, were unsubstantiated claims. The two aircraft destroyed in these combats were Blenheims of Coastal Command.

Case closed. Loud and clear!

Elsewhere, in contrast, Canadians did win successes against the enemy during the day-long battle. Butch Barton of 249 Squadron from North Weald scored a probable against an Me 109, while Ken Lawrence of 234 Squadron from Middle Wallop was credited with damaging an Me 110.

The new German close-escort fighter tactics worked surprisingly well. They would have worked even better had the bombers and fighters been on the same radio wavelength. But although the Messerschmitt 109s, flying well below their top speed, made easier prey for the Hurricanes and Spitfires, the sheer massive scale of the huge formations ensured them getting through to their targets time and time again.

Manston was bombed into a shambles; even its telephone lines were severed. As a forward fuelling base, it ceased to exist and was evacuated. North Weald and Hornchurch fighter fields took a terrific pasting. Southampton and Portsmouth docks were hammered unmercifully. After only a day's experience with the new Luftwaffe tactics, their success had given rise to grave concern by Fighter Command.

Then that night which *The New York Times* described as "one of the greatest miscalculations in history," an incident occurred that changed the course of the battle and the war. In the dark, ten of 170 German bombers over England lost their way. Briefed to bomb the Thameshaven oil installation, they instead dropped their bombs on London. Damage was slight — St. Giles Church at Cripplegate and a statue were hit. But it gave Prime Minister Churchill the excuse he needed to bomb German cities in return, with the certainty that Hitler would retaliate. He knew that the sight of London in flames would kindle American support.

The following night, eighty British bombers struck at Berlin. Now London became the prime target of the Luftwaffe. This deflected the German original bombing plan and altered the tide of the Battle of Britain.

# CHAPTER ELEVEN

# THE IN-HOUSE SQUABBLE

During the last week of August, 1940, only one day went by without a Canadian score. Although the week began rather quietly, on August 25 the RAF lost sixteen fighters. The heaviest losses of the day inflicted by the Luftwaffe was an attack on Warmwell airfield that put it out of action for eighteen hours. Harold Mitchell of 152 Squadron, who was based on that field, nevertheless kept the red ensign flying when he brought down a Messerschmitt 109 with his Spitfire during that afternoon.

The following day was a different story. Canadians rang up a list of nine German aircraft destroyed or damaged, all of them, except one, by No. 1 Fighter Squadron RCAF, which received its indoctrination to combat with the German air force. It also paid a price, posting its first fatality in action.

The focus of the German attack was on Biggin Hill, Hornchurch, Debden and North Weald fighter fields. The Canadians were scrambled at three o'clock that afternoon to intercept the raiders which had been plotted by the controllers enroute to North Weald aerodrome. Climbing to 14,000 feet, they were positioned northeast of the field when the enemy gaggle was sighted, a formation of twenty-five-plus Dornier 215s escorted by Messerschmitt 109s. As Spitfires drew off the enemy fighters, Ernie McNab climbed his squadron to 16,000 feet into the sun like an old pro and dove down — every man for himself.

Picking out the left-hand bomber as his target, he opened fire from 400 yards with a six-second burst of machine-gun fire and closed to 200 yards. In the process, he felt his Hurricane shudder as the Dornier's air-gunner's bullets struck his plane, and he quickly broke off. "I thought my aircraft was on fire," he later recalled. "The cockpit was full of smoke so I got ready to jump." As he flattened out he watched his quarry fall past him and dive into the ground. Then directly ahead he saw an airfield and brought his plane in for a landing.

Attacking with McNab, Bob Edwards of Cobourg, Ont. also destroyed a Dornier. But before doing so his own machine was hit by return fire. Both the Hurricane and the German bomber spun down out of control and crashed into the ground. Edwards thus became the first RCAF pilot to perish in the battle.

Gordie McGregor, leading a section of three in Vic* formation, fired 200 rounds from his Browning machine-guns to bring down another Dornier 215. As he banked away, he saw the crew of two jump out and watched as their parachutes opened.

Vaughan Corbett, the other flight commander, claimed a damaged. His combat report was terse: "Attacked a Do 215 at about 400 yards. I saw smoke issuing from both engines." Credit for another damaged Dornier went to Hartland Molson. "I was Red 2," he recorded, "and on sighting a formation of Do 215s I was ordered into line astern. I attacked one opening fire at about 400 yards and closing to 100. I saw bits flying off the e/a [enemy aircraft], but before completing my attack I had to avoid another e/a falling down out of control directly in my way. After breaking away I was unable to find any other e/a so I returned to base."

Deane Nesbitt and Tommy Little also each damaged one of the bombers in the same combat. Paul Desloges' machine, like McNab's, was damaged by enemy fire. And like his CO, he got away with a forced landing.

Those were not the only Canadian victories that afternoon. Lionel Gaunce celebrated the destruction of his fourth victim destroyed when he shot down an Me 109. But in the same combat his Hurricane was badly shot up.

While Canadians were now heavily engaged in the battle as a whole, another battle was taking place on the inside in which, through no choice or fault of their own, they would become involved. In fact, unbeknown to them, No. 1 RCAF's fighters had already, in a sense, taken part in the affair that has been simmering to a head this very day.

When North Weald, the field that the Canadians had taken off to protect, was attacked two days previous, Keith Park had committed most of his squadrons to engage the enemy before they reached the target. He asked 12 Group to the north to deploy a squadron over the field,

*(V-shaped formation)

but it never arrived. Left unprotected, it was no wonder the aerodrome took such a hammering. Two days later, Park made a similar request to have Debden covered while his fighters attacked the incoming German formations. This time a squadron showed up from Duxford only ten miles away, but it was too late. As a result, the field absorbed a punishing one hundred bombs.

By contrast that afternoon, when his fighters were engaged in trying to stop the German bombers and fighters headed for Portsmouth, Park asked for assistance from Quintin Brand's 10 Group to the west. The response was instantaneous. Three squadrons were dispatched to help the 11 Group fighters. They arrived on the scene so quickly they caught the Heinkel bombers out at sea and forced them to jettison their bombs into the Channel. Brand's group's speedy cooperation saved Portsmouth and its dockyards from further damage sustained two days earlier.

At the heart of the issue between 11 and 12 Groups lay a deep-rooted animosity between its commanders, Park and Trafford Leigh-Mallory, a stubborn type with little or no understanding of air-fighting tactics or strategy. It began in March when Dowding had summoned Leigh-Mallory for an interview. Following the meeting Leigh-Mallory told Park, who was then Dowding's senior Air Staff officer, that he would "move heaven and earth to get Dowding sacked." This infuriated Park who gave Leigh-Mallory a piece of his mind.

Park had twenty-one single-engine fighter squadrons and 250 pilots, resources that most of the time were stretched to the limit. But Dowding had no intention of depleting his other two groups to reinforce 11 Group; its fields and control system could never stand the extra volume. On the other hand, he had given distinct, standing orders that when Park's squadrons were fully engaged the other two groups were to send back-up squadrons when and as requested.

August 27 was a quiet day operationally in which the Luftwaffe limited itself to high-aerial reconnaissance chiefly in the Portsmouth-Southampton area. However, Peter O'Brian, a flight commander with 152 Squadron, when flying a Spitfire from badly battered Warmwell, destroyed his first enemy plane, a Heinkel 111. Still smarting over 12 Group's refusal to protect his fields, Park decided to let fly with full throttle. In his Instruction No. 7 to his controllers, he stated:

> Thanks to the cooperation afforded by 10 Group, they are always prepared to detail two or four squadrons to engage the West mass attacks . . . .
>
> Up to date 12 Group . . . have not shown the same desire to cooperate by dispatching their squadrons to the places requested . . . . When 12

Group offered assistance and were requested by us to patrol our aerodromes, their squadrons did not in fact patrol over our aerodromes . . . .

As . . . direct offers of assistance from 12 Group have not resulted in
their squadrons being placed where we have requested, Controllers are
from now onwards . . . to put their requests to Fighter Command.

Park reported his problems to Dowding, but the commander-in-chief
refused to take sides. In any case, he did not fully understand at the
time, as he admitted later, that Leigh-Mallory's conduct was "a challenge
to my order." Had Park delineated the trouble, he said, he would have
intervened. But it was not until two months later that he decided to
"get rid of Leigh-Mallory."

By that time it was too late. The controversy had already affected RAF
fighter tactics in which many Canadians were totally immersed up to
the top of their flying helmets. And at the highest level, it was to have
sweeping consequences.

# CHAPTER TWELVE

# DECISION

Towards the end of August, 11 Group's pilots were feeling the strain. Tired and often hungry, frequently scrambled just as they started a meal, and flying as many as five patrols a day, they were exhausted. Hammy Hamilton of 85 Squadron was symptomatic of that condition and the fate that habitually accompanied it. Around five o'clock in the afternoon of the 29th, the New Brunswick native had snuck up behind an Me 109 and sent it down in flames to bring his roster of victories up to two-and-a-half planes destroyed, one probable and a damaged. He was feeling pretty pleased with himself, if somewhat weary when, at sixteen minutes after six o'clock, the squadron was scrambled from Croyden again for the fourth time that day.

With Peter Townsend leading, the twelve Hurricanes climbed to 18,000 feet to patrol over Dungeness on the south coast. Out of nowhere a lone Spitfire pulled alongside the formation, waggled its wings and slid to the rear — a stupid, almost criminal, act. End-on, it could have been mistaken for a Messerschmitt 109. It was on a different radio wavelength from the Hurricane so there was no audio communication between them.

When Me 109s did attack, the Spitfire caused such confusion that most of the pilots were taken by surprise. Someone shouted, "Look out! Bandits!" But for Hamilton, it was too late. His aircraft was already heeling over wreathed in flame and smoke taking him to his death in a five-mile plunge to earth.

Townsend was furious. If the Spitfire pilot had stayed on the flank where the pilots could have watched him, Hamilton might never have been killed. In his combat report Townsend stated: "If this Spitfire pilot can be identified I would like these facts brought home to him, because his . . . actions contributed to the loss of one of my flight commanders." It was just as pertinent, though, that Hamilton had possibly lost his fine edge of alertness due to combat fatigue. In either case, or both, a good pilot had been lost, and at this stage good, seasoned pilots were hard to come by.

RAF fighter strength was dwindling and the Germans sensed it. After a flight over England, Kurt von Doering, one of the Luftwaffe's fighter leaders, categorically claimed "unlimited fighter superiority over the RAF." Despite the Herculean efforts of Beaverbrook, Fighter Command was losing more planes than it was getting. Replacement of pilots had reached a crisis stage, too, whereby flyers were being brought in from other commands — bomber and coastal — neither trained nor particularly suited temperamentally for fighters. Others were arriving fresh from training school with only a few hours of operational instruction. Many of the squadrons were rapidly reaching the point where they would soon cease to be of front-line calibre.

But the Germans had problems, too. A reorganization had given Luftflotte 3, under Hugo Sperrle, responsibility for night bombing raids which at first were largely unsuccessful. The bomber crews were having a tough time finding their targets without radio directional finding aids. Luftflotte 2, under "Smiling Albert" Kesselring, tackled the daylight attacks. His crews were even more overworked than Park's airmen, but Kesselring was as much an optimist as Goering was unrealistic. Neither of them understood that fatigue resulted in heavy losses.

On August 30, a day in which Fighter Command flew over 1,000 sorties for the first time, the main focal point was Biggin Hill, the lynchpin of the fighter defences guarding London. Two different attacks, one in the morning and the other after lunch when Park had every one of his fighters in the air, wrecked workshops, stores, hangars, severed gas and water mains, and killed or wounded sixty-five station personnel.

But there was a brighter side, and it was Canadian to the core. At Coltishall that morning with such a drain on 11 Group, 242 Squadron was ordered south to Duxford. After a recall it once again set off for the field just north of London. Then shortly after four o'clock the phone rang and a voice barked: "Laycock Squadron Scramble! Angels fifteen. North Weald."

Douglas Bader led his Hurricanes west of the field to position them at 21,000 feet when suddenly George Christie spotted a mixed bag of Messerschmitt 110s and Heinkel 111s heading towards North Weald aerodrome from the east. They were stepped up in two layers, a now-familiar pattern in use by the Luftwaffe at 14,000 and 20,000 feet.

Christie's section tackled the upper layer, diving in to break up the German formation. Christie attacked one of the enemy fighters head-on, a highly risky practice in the face of the 110's powerful armament of two cannons and four machine-guns in the nose. But the enemy pilot broke to the right and went into a dive with the Hurricane in hot pursuit. From a range of fifty yards, Christie delivered a series of successive bursts from his eight Browning guns. Oil started to spew from the Messerschmitt's starboard engine and then the fuel tank exploded. From 8,000 feet the aircraft went into a vertical dive and crashed into a greenhouse near Ponders' End.

Meanwhile, Norrie Hart attacked three Heinkel 111s from above, singling out one which went into a dive. Hart let it go and picked another Heinkel, giving it a long steady burst that sent it down in flames.

Noel Stansfeld and another pilot sighted a straggling He 111 to the east. On his first pass Stansfeld noticed the rear-gunner's weapon "twinkling like a flashlight going on and off." But its bullets went awry and Stansfeld soon silenced it. He then set the port engine on fire. Suddenly the other engine simply stopped and the bomber crashed into a field strewn with wrecked cars to thwart enemy parachute landings.

Willie McKnight's performance was the most spectacular of all. The sharpshooter from Edmonton zeroed in on the middle section of the ME 110s. As two of them broke away, McKnight got behind another. Opening fire from 100 yards, he sent the enemy aircraft crashing to the ground in flames.

He next attacked a Heinkel formation from the beam, again getting in close before pressing the firing button. At 150 yards' range he struck the bomber putting the port engine out of commission and sending the machine rolling over on its back. Suddenly, it began to smoke, then caught fire and spiralled into a field.

McKnight scored his third victory of the outing after being attacked by an Me 110 which, by twisting and turning, he got behind. The enemy pilot displayed extreme dexterity at the controls of a twin-engine machine by pulling into steep turns allowing the rear-gunner to take aim on the attacker. But the manoeuvres were no match for the Hurricane. Finally the enemy straightened out and McKnight fired from such close range — thirty yards — that he could almost have reached out and touched the Messerschmitt. The starboard engine caught fire, and the aircraft crashed near a reservoir.

After the squadron flew back to Coltishall that evening, McKnight wrote laconically in his log book: "Squadron 'Bag' — 12. Personal — 3. 2 Me 110s, 1 He 111. Confirmed Total — 17."

A message from the chief of the Air Staff, Cyril Newall, to the squadron was exuberant by contrast: "Magnificent fighting. You are well on top of the enemy. And obviously the fine Canadian traditions of the last war are safe in your hands."

But Douglas Bader was far from satisfied. When Leigh-Mallory congratulated him on a good show, Bader complained that if he'd had a wing of three squadrons to lead he could have accounted for three times as many of the enemy. A good thought, Leigh-Mallory agreed, one to mull over and discuss with his superior, the deputy chief of Air Staff, Sholto Douglas. Volatile high-octane fuel was about to added to a bonfire already ablaze.

That afternoon, Hitler came to one decision and made another. He postponed setting a date for the invasion of England until September 10 because he did not consider "the prerequisites for Sea Lion fulfilled, judging from the present progress of the war in the air . . . " even though the Luftwaffe reported that "the British fighter defence is severely crippled." But if logic had overruled optimism on the one hand, embarrassment and rage took over on the other. Goering had promised that he would change his name to "Meir" if British bombs landed on Germany. To Alfred Jodl, OKW chief of staff, Hitler announced: "I now give permission for large-scale reprisal attacks on London."

# CHAPTER THIRTEEN

# BLACK DAY

The last day of August, 1940, turned out to be the blackest one of the entire battle for the RAF. The Germans flew 1,300 sorties to protect their bombers on a series of successful attacks on the British fighter fields south of London. The RAF lost thirty-nine fighters, reaching parity with enemy losses of forty-one. Thirteen of Hugh Dowding's precious pilots were killed. Now he could no longer afford to rotate his squadrons.

Ironically, the day was another banner one for the Canadians, for the second time in a row. No. 1 Fighter Squadron RCAF scored three aircraft destroyed and two damaged. Other Canadian victors were two pilots flying with the RAF who accounted for another enemy plane destroyed and one damaged. On the debit side, four planes were lost although all the aircrew parachuted to safety — three of them before breakfast. At 8:30 a.m., the Canadian squadron was again scrambled to intercept a formation of one hundred aircraft headed for Dover. Once again communications, or a lack of them, played a part in the unit's action. When Keith Park learned that the enemy gaggle was made up of Me 109s, he instantly recalled the Hurricane squadrons that had been sent up. But the RCAF pilots never got the signal. In any case, the formation consisted of Dornier 215 and Heinkel 111 bombers escorted not by Me 109s but by 110s.

Bounced by a Staffel of the twin-engine fighters from out of the sun, Bill Sprenger, Vaughan Corbett and George Hyde never even saw what hit them before they bailed out. Sprenger landed at Staplehurst, Hyde at Wildershaw railway station and Corbett in a field nearby. Both Corbett and Hyde suffered face, hand and leg burns, but Sprenger alighted none the worse for wear.

Meanwhile, Roland Dibnah from No. 1 Squadron RAF, also stationed at Northolt, latched onto the tail of a 110 over Chelmsford which was trailing the enemy formation. Dibnah made an initial pass, dove, then climbed his Hurricane steeply to make a quarter-beam attack on the leading aircraft of a section of three. He gave it a burst between 800 and 400 yards and noticed black smoke streaming from the starboard engine. Though it never broke formation, Dibnah was credited with a damaged.

At the same time, Jimmy Cochrane and his 257 Squadron, flying Hurricanes from its advanced base at Martlesham Heath which had been repaired and was now back in service, tangled with fifty Me 110s that went into a defensive circle over Clacton. Cochrane fired several long bursts at one of them and saw two crew members take to their parachutes.

These actions, however, failed to deter the Germans from plastering Croydon, Biggin Hill and Hornchurch with bombs from 12,000 feet. On the latter field, a squadron of Spitfires was caught on the ground taking off — the scenario all pilots dreaded — as the missiles rained down. Fortunately, the two "Maple Leaf" squadrons — Nos. 1 RCAF and 242 RAF, with their bases at Northolt on the far side of London, and Coltishall to the north — were well out of the prime airfield attack zone, sparing them the dangers of these concentrated raids.

Later in the day, a delegation from No. 1 buried its first casualty, Bob Edwards, killed five days earlier. The rest of the pilots remained on readiness. Then at 5:30 p.m., the squadron was scrambled again.

This time the pilots encountered a formation of Junkers 88s escorted by Me 109s and 110s at 12,000 feet over Gravesend, east of London and south of the Thames. The Canadians immediately sailed into the enemy, and although their own anti-aircraft fire somewhat hampered their attacks, before the mêlée ended a few moments later two Me 109s and a Dornier 215 had been destroyed, and another 109 and a 215 damaged. The only casualty was Jean Desloges, the former Mountie, who was forced to jump when his Hurricane caught fire.

The squadron's subsequent combat reports zipped with the drama of the action:

> I saw two Me 109s below and to the right. I got on the tail of the right-hand one and fired a burst of seven seconds starting at 250 yards and closing to 150. The e/a started to smoke, flames bursting out on both sides of the fuselage, and it nosed down into a field and burnt up. I fired a short burst at the second Me 109, the first rounds going wide and he half-rolled into a dive.
>
> -Bev Christmas

> I climbed to 25,000 feet and sighted a Do 215 at 17,000 feet near the Estuary of the Thames moving very sluggishly. I overtook the e/a rapidly

and dove, firing about 25 rounds at a range of 300 yards. The e/a went into a dive and plunged into the sea about five miles from the shore.

-Johnny Kerwin

I saw an Me 109 cross in front of me and begin a turn to the right. I followed and got inside his turn and fired a long burst of about ten seconds at a range of 200 yards. The e/a started to smoke and break up. I saw a ball of fire break off and the pilot bail out.

-Tommy Little

I opened fire at 350 yards and closed to 100 yards with three short bursts of about 50 rounds each. On my second and third bursts, pieces started to fall off the tail of the e/a and he slowed down and lagged behind. I broke away so violently that I lost sight of the bombers . . .

-Dal Russel

I followed in rear of the bombers hoping to get in an attack when I noticed an Me 109 firing at me from my left. I swung around in a tight turn and got a short deflection shot at about 400 yards. Smoke started to appear from behind the engine and in front of the cockpit, and he went into a spiral turn, smoking badly.

-Ross Smither

Such exuberance did not extend to the command level. In addition to the thirty-nine aircraft lost in combat, ten Spitfires had been destroyed on the ground. One of Park's squadrons had been so badly beaten up it had to be retired to a quiet sector for re-manning and re-equipping.

Practically every one of the airfields south of London had been damaged, some of them temporarily out of commission. All Goering had to do was knock out Kenley and Tangmere to make further air defence of southeast England almost impossible.

# CHAPTER FOURTEEN

# ZEILWECHSEL

For the next three days, the Luftwaffe continued to hammer away at the sector fields, and the Allies' situation had now become desperate. Since July 1, forty-six squadron leaders had been lost, and thirty-nine of the ninety-six flight commanders had been killed or wounded. Experienced pilots were at a premium. "Sprogs" reporting to the squadrons had less than twenty-four hours' experience on Hurricanes and Spitfires. Poor tactics on the part of Allied fighter squadrons didn't help, either.

The RAF still clung to the unwieldy, tight "Vic" sections of three aircraft. Pilots on the flanks had to concentrate on staying in formation while spotting in any direction mainly depended on the leader who called the shots. Once the "Tally Ho" was given, the wingmates would automatically, or on order, fall into line-astern for the attack. If the target was a bomber, should the enemy gunner live long enough he might miss number one, but had an opportunity to get a hit on number two, and was almost certain to score against number three. Once a mêlée began, everyone had to look out for himself. But it was the spotting, and being spotted, that counted first.

In this the Germans were at a great advantage due to the flexibility of their fighter sections. During the Spanish Civil War, the Luftwaffe pilots had developed the supple *Schwarm* formation comprised of a loose grouping of two pairs each looking out for his partner's tail.

The Germans had also abandoned the clumsy close-escort fighter protection concept in favour of stepped-up formations of bombers and fighters in several layers. This stretched the Allied defenders' problems of coping with the German fighters at different heights, although 11 Group commander Keith Park's instructions were to concentrate mainly on the bombers.

It is to the credit of the Allied fighter pilots (and their commanders) that they were able to cope so well with such cumbersome tactics. Hartland

Molson once told me: "We really knew nothing in those early days." But cope they did, and in noble fashion. Early on in the afternoon of September 1, using their Vic-to-Line-Astern deployment in four different sections, No. 1 RCAF Squadron broke up a formation of Dorniers south-west of Croydon with a head-on attack from 2,000 feet above, coming out of the sun, that resulted in one of the bombers being shot down, another probably destroyed and three damaged. In addition, one of the escorting fighters was sent to its doom.

Gordie McGregor saw his tracers strike a Do 215 which pulled up, obviously stricken. Then, switching his attention to another one of the Dorniers, he made a quick quarter-beam deflection attack that sent the aircraft diving earthward. Because he lost sight of it, he only claimed a probable.

Ed Reyno, Bev Christmas and Tommy Little shared in the damage of another bomber, and Otto Peterson also claimed a damaged. But Johnny Kerwin turned in the star performance. In the mass head-on attack, he fired seventy rounds into one of the enemy machines that sent it spinning into the ground. Then he spotted eight Messerschmitt 110s chasing two Hurricanes and gave chase. Singling out the rear German fighter, he fired what was the last of his ammunition into it. At that moment cannon-fire pierced his auxiliary fuel tank causing a fire in the cockpit. Kerwin wasted no time jumping over the side and parachuted into a farmer's field near Maidstone. Except for face and hand burns, he escaped serious injury.

Over the next two days, Canadians flying with other squadrons continued to add to the country's laurels. On September 2, Butch Barton, while flying a Hurricane with 249 Squadron from North Weald, shared in shooting down a Dornier 215, while Arthur Trueman with 253 Squadron, who would meet his demise two days later, damaged an Me 109. On September 3, Jack Carpenter illustrated how critical Fighter Command's need for pilots had become. A native of Toronto, he had been seconded to the RAF from the Royal Naval Fleet Air Army. Dowding was near the end of his tether. That day Camille Bonseigneur of Regina, a pilot with 257 Hurricane Squadron, was added to the growing list of Canadian casualties.

Across the Channel that morning, an OKW Command directive read: "The earliest date for the invasion fleet's departure had been fixed at September 20, landing on September 21." Seventeen days to go. No time to lose. The pressure was on the Luftwaffe to knock out the RAF fighter force — in double-quick time. But how? And in which direction? To Luftflotte 3 commander, Hugo Sperrle, the answer was obvious: Keep clobbering the fighter fields. A week should do the trick. Easily.

Albert Kesselring, the Luftflotte 2 commander, disagreed. Now that Hitler had given permission to bomb London, the British capital should be attacked without mercy. This was more to the liking of the bloodthirsty Goering. Had he been any kind of strategist, however, he should have listened to Sperrle, an airman and a bombing specialist, and not Kesselring who, although he had bombed Warsaw and Rotterdam into submission, was still very much a soldier at heart and despite his gregarious mien was more of a sadist than a realist. ("When we knock a few cockney heads, they'll soon give in.")

The die was cast in any case. At the opening of the *Winterhilfe* — winter relief fund — in the Berlin Sportsplast next afternoon, Hitler announced the main *Zeilwechsel* — target switch — to London. Before a frenzied crowd he proclaimed: "Mr. Churchill is demonstrating his new brainchild, the night air raid. . . . For three weeks I did not answer because I believed that such madness would be stopped. . . . When they declare they will increase their attacks on our cities, then we will raze their cities to the ground."

Italian foreign minister, Count Ciano, listening to the speech on the radio, commented: "Hitler must be nervous." Certainly his nerves played a part in the fatal decision to switch the Luftwaffe's winning attacks on the RAF to bombing London. That decision came in part out of revenge for the bombings of Berlin, but mostly because Hitler earnestly believed that by flattening their capital the British will to resist would be broken, and an invasion, which Hitler actually dreaded, would not be necessary. The Fuehrer too should have listened to Sperrle.

Meanwhile, another factor intervened. Based on faulty Intelligence reports that British aircraft output was exceeding fighter losses, on September 4 Goering ordered the factories bombed, splitting his forces even more between those raids and the others on the aerodromes. Inevitably, a lot of sting went out of the attacks on the latter.

In the morning the Germans hit at the Kentish airfields and then later bombed the Vickers plant at Brooklands and the Short Bros. factory at Rochester; both, ironically, bomber manufacturers. At Northolt the press arrived and were in the process of interviewing and photographing when a scramble order came at one o'clock and twelve Hurricanes from No. 1 Fighter Squadron RCAF took the air. Members of the fourth estate were duly impressed with the efficiency and speed of the take-off. They had even more to write about when the Canadians landed forty minutes later.

Twenty minutes after becoming airborne, the Hurricane pilots had reached 18,000 feet over East Grinstead when they sighted a swarm of Me 110s 3,000 feet below them. As they dove from out of the sun, the

Messerschmitts went into their customary defensive circle to spread the fire. The German fighters were flying anti-clockwise and the Canadians curved into the circle from the opposite direction.

Ross Smither got in a fast deflection shot from 400 yards and his target fell out of the formation. Opening fire on a second machine from a ninety-degree angle, he set it on fire. Deane Nesbitt sent another one of the 110s down in flames. Hartland Molson managed to damage two more of the enemy fighters and Gordie McGregor fired on one of them, seeing pieces break off it as it banked away apparently out of control.

Otto Peterson took careful aim on another Me 110, coming in from the rear quarter. Smoke started to pour from the starboard engine and the rear-gunner stopped firing. Then a piece flew off the fin. Peterson kept shooting, seeing his tracers strike the fuselage. The aircraft appeared to wobble just as another Me 110 attacked him from below. Peterson broke off downwards, pulling up so sharply he blacked out. Outside the circle, Dal Russel, in tandem with Eric Beardmore, tackled a Junkers 88 which appeared below them. Opening fire, his bullets struck the port engine which began to smoke and then he broke off. Russel then attacked an Me 110, following it out to sea but lost it. As he turned for home he saw a rescue launch chuffing in the direction where he figured the Messerschmitt could have gone into the water.

But those weren't the only successes for the Canadians that day. Ken Lawrence, serving with 234 Squadron, damaged an Me 110 while George Christie, now sporting a DFC under his wings, shot down a 109 and was given credit for probably destroying another. Maple Leaf tally for the day: three destroyed, two probables and six damaged. Tragically, Arthur Trueman of 257 Squadron was killed in action.

*          *          *

Based on that day's performance by the Luftwaffe, Park decided to divide his fighters between protecting the aircraft factories and the key sector fields. On September 5, twenty-two different German formations attacked these targets within eight hours. In the midst of these raids, John Boyle of 41 Squadron destroyed an Me 109, as did Jack Carpenter, the transplanted navy pilot, while Roland Dibnah, one of Bader's pilots, brought down a 110.

Boyle's combat report illustrated the intensity of the day's fighting:

> I was Green 3 . . . patrolling between Maidstone and Ramsgate. Interception was made at 20,000 feet; enemy aircraft varying from 16,000 to 22,000 feet. Green Section attacked bombers [Do 17s] in line-astern formation. Seven or eight Me 109s were covering these bombers. Three Me 109s came in between me and Green 1 and 2. I attacked the most

convenient e/a, starting to fire from above with quarter deflection closing in to dead-astern. A four- or five-second burst was enough. The 109 broke up, with flame and smoke coming from the right-hand side; it immediately rolled on its back and spun.

Dibnah's unit, 242 Squadron, had been practising take-offs and landings, and forming up with two other squadrons from Duxford. The exercise had Leigh-Mallory's full blessing as well as the hearty approval of the deputy chief of the Air Staff, Sholto Douglas. Bader had reduced squadron take-off time to three minutes, but the Wing still had to form up. Keith Park of 11 Group was not against the "Big Wing" formations per se. Far from it. At the time of Dunkirk, he had initiated their use in formations as large as four squadrons. But that was for offensive purposes when there was lots of time to form up. Not so easily done defensively.

Rarely was it possible to detect the enemy's intentions until it reached the coast, about twenty minutes' flying time from the centre of London. It took all that time and more for the British fighters to reach 20,000 feet, so they had to be off the ground and climbing in a flash. For that reason Park, for the most part, confined his formations to single squadrons, two at the most, although on rare occasions this was increased to three.

Hugh Dowding said later that had Big Wings been used by 11 Group, a great many more enemy bombers would have reached their targets. Park was even more explicit: "Had I tried Bader's theories of the Big Wing," he said, "I would have lost the Battle of Britain."

Leigh-Mallory could have cared less about overall strategy. Just because his group wasn't on the front line didn't mean that he wasn't going to get his share of battle honours. Besides, he had his eye on Park's job which he thought should have been his in the first place. It went to Park because of his experience; he was a twenty-plane ace from the First World War, had commanded Tangmere fighter station and had worked as Dowding's senior staff officer. When WWII began, he was regarded as the RAF's foremost expert on fighters. Leigh-Mallory, who had also been attached to Dowding's staff, although a WWI ace as well (five planes to his credit), his expertise was army cooperation reconnaissance. But he had commanded 12 Group since 1937 and outranked Park, so he felt he should have got the call. But this was no "It's my turn" peacetime sort of promotion. This was war. And by comparison with Park he lacked the calibre and fighter savvy needed to take over the most vital group of them all. However, Leigh-Mallory resented having to play second-fiddle and, by September, it was beginning to show.

September 6 saw a renewed attack on the British aircraft industry and a continuation of fighter-field assaults. The Hawker works at Kingston, which produced half the output of Hurricanes, was hard hit. Canada posted a lone victory that day when Hilly Brown, now wearing the DFC, damaged a Junkers 88. That morning photographic reconnaissance machines provided evidence of the German invasion fleet in the Channel ports. A landing on England, it seemed, could not be far off.

Even with the focus of German raids on the aircraft plants, Fighter Command in the south of England was reeling. Six of 11 Group's sector fields and five advanced aerodromes were severely damaged. Fighter losses in the previous two weeks exceeded production by nearly 200. During August, 300 pilots had been killed or wounded.

Of all this the average British citizen, who was still to feel the brunt of the war, was almost casually unaware, apart from rationing and other shortcomings. At times he or she could see the battle raging above. Quite colourful as a matter of fact. Occasionally they would witness a pilot — Allied or German — landing by parachute. Interesting. Often bombs burst uncomfortably close by, damaged houses, scared animals. Bloody nuisance. There were other inconveniences, but Britons happily adjusted to them. St. Melon's Golf Club amended its rules to suit circumstances: "A ball lying in a crater may be dropped . . . A player whose stroke is affected by the . . . explosion of a bomb . . . or by machine-gun fire may play another ball . . . penalty one stroke." All in good spirit. But the harsh realities of enemy aerial bombardment were now about to be suddenly brought home to them.

Even though the cost to the Luftwaffe had been critical — Kesselring's fleet had been reduced to 450 bombers and 530 fighters — victory was still within grasp. Then, abruptly, the Germans launched operation "*Loge*" — so-called after the god who had forged Siegfried's sword — the Blitz on London.

# CHAPTER FIFTEEN

# BIG WING

On September 7, the Duxford Wing went into battle for the first time as a unified squad. In mid-afternoon, Goering hurled 348 bombers and 617 fighters against London in a single massive blow. Park, having to scramble every fighter available, sent a call to 12 Group for support. Shortly after 5:00 p.m., 242 and two squadrons from Duxford took off with instructions to climb to 10,000 feet and patrol over Middle Wallop. But Douglas Bader wanted to take his covey higher than that to get the height advantage. However, by the time the pilots spotted the enemy formation — some ninety bombers in box formation escorted by more than 100 Messerschmitt 109s and 110s — the Germans were well above them. Nevertheless, climbing at full throttle and maximum boost, the Duxford Wing charged into them.

Within seconds, aircraft were scattered all over the sky as if this was the confrontation everyone had been waiting for, three Canadians prominent among them. Hugh Tamblyn got on the tail of an Me 110 and gave it a five-second burst from 200 yards that set it on fire just as a 109 bounced him from above. Yanking into a steep right-hand turn, he pulled up behind the Messerschmitt and from 150 yards took a shot at it. The German fighter nosed down smoking, dove, climbed, then floundered about and disappeared. Later Tamblyn would claim a probable. But right now his adrenaline was flowing in fine pitch and he began firing at everything in sight, an impulsiveness he soon regretted.

Suddenly several Me 109 stragglers appeared below him in an ideal position for him to shoot them down. He pressed the trigger only to hear a pneumatic hiss of air; he'd run out of ammunition. He wasn't the only one who had wasted bullets, however. When he landed, his mechanics whistled in disbelief. His Hurricane had taken a hit in the port wing and seven bullets in the starboard wing!

Noel Stansfeld, meanwhile, had stalked a Dornier 215, encountering defensive fire from the rear-gunner whose aim, fortunately for him, went amiss. When he drew within 300 yards of his target, Stansfeld opened fire from the left beam underneath. Keeping his thumb on the firing button he closed to within fifty yards. The German bomber rolled over twice, then hurtled straight into the ground.

Stan Turner, leading a section of three Hurricanes, was the last of his squadron to join in the fracas. Picking out an Me 110, he opened fire just as a 109 jumped him from behind, forcing him to break into the attack. Manoeuvring onto the enemy's tail, he got home a solid burst that sent the aircraft into a steep dive. Then another Me 109 bounced him and he had to take evasive action again. For all his pains Turner survived the hectic struggle with merely a damaged Me 109 to his credit.

On this occasion, the use of the Big Wing had been overwhelmingly impressive. One fighting unit had accounted for twenty enemy aircraft shot down, six probably destroyed, and eight damaged — a total of thirty-four planes that never reached the target. Bader lost only one of his pilots — John Benzie, a native Winnipegger. But did this mean a successful outcome? Not necessarily. Of the aircraft destroyed, only three were bombers — the very aircraft Park had ordered his 11 Group squadrons (in much smaller and less unwieldy formations) to concentrate on in an effort to prevent them from reaching their targets and dropping their bombs, which was the main Luftwaffe objective. On the other side of the coin, it could be argued that diminishing German fighter strength was not an entirely unproductive achievement either, even if it was not the prime purpose of the role of the defender.

On this same date, Skeets Ogilvie, a Spitfire pilot with 609 Squadron stationed at Middle Wallop, was on a roll of his own running up his first score against the enemy. While on patrol at 10,000 feet between Brooklands and Windsor, the squadron spotted 200 enemy aircraft over London surrounded by anti-aircraft fire. The Spitfires climbed towards them and, in the tussle that followed, Ogilvie downed an Me 109 and probably destroyed an He 110. Another Canadian double-winner that day was Ken Lawrence, who destroyed one Me 109 and damaged another.

Over Rochester, Jimmy Cochrane's 257 Squadron intercepted fifty German Dornier 215 bombers flying up the Thames Estuary. But escorting Messerschmitt fighters quickly broke up the Hurricanes' attack. The British Columbian became separated from his mates when his engine momentarily conked out. A few minutes later he caught a lone Dornier heading homeward and dove on it from out of the sun. Breaking off at close range, he pulled up and was about to open fire again when the bomber began to belch smoke and the crew of three bailed out into the sea. Glittering metallic strips dangled from their parachutes as they fluttered down, apparently to distinguish them from British parachutists. It so fascinated Cochrane that he stayed in the vicinity for half an hour to direct a rescue launch to pick up the enemy flyers.

Shortly after six o'clock that evening, Ernie McNab was flying in company with a Spitfire towards Maidstone when five yellow-nosed Messerschmitt 109s, flying in line-astern, shot in front of him 2,000 feet below. "I attacked the rear one with a deflection shot," McNab said later, "and followed into line-astern using my excess height to follow them. The enemy fighter ahead of me climbed and I fired a 150 bullets from each gun from a range of 150 yards. Then it suddenly climbed vertically and fell straight down." McNab got a glimpse of white vapour pouring from the fuselage before he broke off, claiming a probable.

That night bombs rained down on the world's largest metropolis. Ironically, it had been a quarter of a century earlier on September 15, 1915, that the Kaiser's Zeppelins made their first major raid on London. On September 7/8, 1940, from eight o'clock in the evening until five o'clock the following morning, a continuous stream of Hitler's bombers dropped 330 tons of explosives and 440 canisters of incendiaries on the city. By dawn, 306 Londoners had been killed and 1,337 wounded, most of them severely.

At Fighter Command, the change in Luftwaffe tactics brought about a mild sense of relief. It had eased the pressure on the hard-hit sector stations, but it could do nothing to increase the flow of new fighter pilots to replace the losses of August and the first week of September. And there was still the imminent danger of invasion.

Hugh Dowding now reclassified his squadrons into three categories: (1) those in 11 Group and its immediate flanks who would bear the brunt of the fighting; (2) a small number at operational strength who would provide immediate relief when needed; and (3) remaining units, stripped of their operational pilots for category one, to be used for training. This indicated how desperately Dowding's resources had been stretched. Standing patrols could no longer be maintained, and it was largely believed that paratroops would be used to occupy the sector fields which were now provided with extra anti-aircraft batteries.

Luckily, the day after the change in Luftwaffe targets turned out to be a quiet one, partly due to duff weather. Jack Carpenter of 46 Squadron "bought it," the eleventh Canadian fatality in the battle. But that night another 207 bombers struck at London leaving 412 dead and 747 badly injured. Next day, September 9, the Londoners could take some consolation only in the fact that Fighter Command repelled a daylight attack on the city. And in this fighting, which took place shortly after five o'clock in the afternoon, Canadians racked up a total of seven aircraft destroyed and four damaged.

Willie McKnight sent one Me 109 to its doom in flames and another crashing into the ground. But in the skirmish his own left aileron was shot away although he managed to land safely.

John Latta's aircraft also sustained damage in a scrap with a 109 which he set on fire. He managed to get back to Duxford where he set down his aircraft all in one piece.

Hugh Tamblyn was a double-winner setting two Me 110s on fire, the second of which crashed into a cricket clubhouse. During the fracas Bader lost another of his Canadians, Kirkpatrick Schlanders from Newfoundland.

Otto Peterson, who blew an Me 109 to bits, Pete Lochnan, who severely damaged two Messerschmitts, and Ernie McNab, who mauled another 109, posted scores for the RCAF. Peterson's attack was so fierce and at such close range that fragments of glass and Perspex cut his face open and blood obscured his vision. Unable to read his instruments, he fell to 1,500 feet before he was able to recover. In the same combat, Bill Millar of Penticton was forced to bail out with a wounded leg and burns to his face.

George Corbett of Victoria, flying a Spitfire with 66 Squadron, got into a scrap with a 109 which he claimed as a probable having seen vapour steaming out the engine after a sustained burst of fire. He then tangled with another 109 which got the better of him. A cannon-shell that exploded under the seat filled the cockpit with smoke. The control column jumped out of his hand then jammed into the far left corner, sending the aircraft into a tight spiral downwards. At 12,000 feet Corbett abandoned ship and parachuted safely into a field near Cowden.

Johnny Kent, leading his Poles in concert with Ernie McNab's outfit, accounted for an Me 110 which he shot down into the sea, and a damaged Junkers 88. Later he chronicled this colourful account of his encounter.

> The light was poor, so I set off towards the French coast hoping I might find the damaged bomber when, quite unexpectedly, I saw a twin-engined aircraft that, at first, looked like a Hampden. As I got closer it began to look less than familiar and then its rear-gunner opened fire, so even though it was not the Ju 88 I was looking for, I immediately attacked. It was quite fascinating and made a pretty sight in the gloom watching

my tracers sail gracefully towards the German while at the same time his came streaming back at me like a string of gleaming beads.

After my third burst, the enemy made a sharp turn to port and the silhouette it presented was that of an Me 110. I can remember the picture so terribly clearly; it was like a picture out of a book on air firing — "at this angle place your sights there and FIRE" — which is what I did, and his starboard engine flew to bits . . .

On landing at Northholt, in the excitement of having won his first victory, he nearly took Stuffy Dowding's head off with his wingtip while taxiing in. Fortunately, the Fighter Command C-in-C, on a visit to the station, ducked just in time. When a red-faced Kent hastened to apologize for forcing such an exalted personage to bow to him, Dowding replied good-naturedly, "Under the circumstances I was only too happy to oblige . . . "

That night, both Kent's and McNab's pilots could hear the German bombers droning overhead. Sperrle's Luftflotte 3 had quickly established a technique of coming over in small waves at intervals along clearly defined corridors of approach using different routes on the way home. In the raid another 370 Londoners were killed and a further 1,700 wounded. The next day, September 10, saw a lull in German activity although that evening London was again hit hard. This was a plight that London's stalwart citizens had already begun to almost philosophically accept as routine, taking to mattressing in the cellar or sleeping in the station platforms of the Tube, the city's subway system. "London Can Take It," Fleet Street proclaimed proudly.

Although the air raids satisfied Hitler's thirst for retaliation, he was realistic enough to understand that without smothering the RAF fighter force an invasion of England could never succeed. Fighter Command had proved to be a tougher nut to crack than his Luftwaffe leaders, including Goering, had led him to believe. He again postponed making a decision to launch Operation Sea Lion until September 14. In truth he never had much faith in the invasion fleet, in any case. Not that it mattered. He was still firmly convinced that sustained raids on London would crush the British will to resist in short order, forcing a quick peace, and making an invasion unnecessary anyway.

# CHAPTER SIXTEEN

# HIGH-WATER MARK

The date is September 11. The voice is Churchill's. The message is strident.

> If this invasion is going to be tried at all, it does not seem that it can be long delayed. . . . Therefore, we must regard the next week or so as a very important period in our history. It ranks with the days when the Spanish Armada was approaching the Channel and Drake was finishing his game of bowls; or when Nelson stood between us and Napoleon's Grand Army at Boulogne. We have read about this in the history books; but what is happening now is on a far greater scale and of more consequence to the life and future of the world and its civilization than these great days of the past.

Lofty words of a lofty time. Stirring, backbone-stiffening stuff. But fighter pilots were not among the audience. Such uplifting rhetoric was wasted on them. Ensconced in a small world of their own, and barely aware of the great issues at stake, they were singularly unmoved by it. Nor could they have cared less. They had their own problems. As Eric Beardmore, put it: "We had a job to do, shooting down Huns and that was it. I didn't worry about any German invasion. My biggest concern was whether that bloody blower would go off and I'd have to run for my kite before I could finish my breakfast."

Live for today. Let tomorrow take care of itself. In general, a good life. Hectic, risky and often short. But, what the hell?

By nature the fighter pilots treated their lot — and their fate — with a certain carefree indifference. They were not involved in the intimate slaughter of close combat on the battlefield. Shooting down an enemy aircraft was impersonal, even though its occupant might die hideously. Air-fighting was more in the nature of a sport if, indeed, a terribly deadly one. Triumph brought immense satisfaction; destroying an enemy plane was tantamount to kicking Goering in the teeth. Dowding said later that his "Chicks," as Churchill called them, tended to treat everything as if "it was all a big joke." Certainly with a cheerful irreverence, anyway. When the British prime minister paid them his famous tribute that "Never in the field of human conflict was so much owed by so many to so few," one Canadian Spitfire pilot remarked ruefully, "He must be talking about our liquor bills."

Still, for Fighter Command, and in particular the Canadian pilots within it, Churchill's prognostications that the next seven days would prove to be the most stirring, eventful and consequential weeks in history was not without foundation or extraordinary foresight.

For in that period, during which the Battle of Britain would be decided, Canadian fighter pilots could claim approximately twenty-six aircraft shot down, five probably destroyed and ten damaged, with five of those destroyed, three of them probables and five of them damaged, credited to the RCAF. All this at a remarkably light downside of only two Canadians killed.

For openers the RCAF took the lead. On Wednesday, the first day of that notorious week, Kesselring launched the third daylight raid on London since September 7. At four o'clock in the afternoon, in weather that remained mainly clear, No. 1 Canadian Squadron RCAF, led by Ernie McNab, was scrambled to intercept a formation of twenty-plus Heinkel 111 bombers covered by a swarm of Messerschmitt 109 fighters above them.

Fifteen minutes later, from 18,000 feet, the Hurricane pilots who were joined by Spitfires of 41 Squadron that had taken off from Rochford, spotted the herd of enemy aircraft southeast of Gatwick flying in a southerly direction 4,000 feet below them. The Spitfire pilots tackled the fighters while McNab's Hurricanes plowed into the midst of the Heinkels.

"The McNab" was first into the fray. Ordering his squadron into port echelon — each section stepped back in tiers to the left — he led his numbers two and three, Pete Lochnan and Bev Christmas, in a right-beam attack on the top group of Heinkels. McNab opened fire at a twenty-degree angle drawing in behind the bomber. As he banked aside, the starboard engine belched smoke. Following in behind him, Lochnan took aim but a burst from the Heinkel's rear-gunner struck his Hurricane. His aircraft's engine faltering, Lochnan started down in a shallow dive looking for the nearest field in which to force-land. Christmas swept in from the other side, taking a four-second burst from 400 yards. His bullets put the rear-gunner out of business and the port engine began to smoke.

But that merely left the fate of the Heinkel uncertain, because none of the three Canadians saw any further result. McNab and Christmas claimed only a damaged between them.

Meanwhile, from up-sun Red Section leader Gordie McGregor marshalled his numbers two and three, Deane Nesbitt and Hartland Molson, into line-astern for a diving attack on the bombers' starboard flank. All three Canadians got in good deflection shots, although none scored a hit, and then swerved to the right. As McGregor levelled out, he came face to face with a lone Heinkel. Although one of its engines seemed to be smoking slightly, the plane somehow maintained its height and speed. McGregor swooped in from the port quarter, drew a bead on the bomber and had just commenced firing when another Hurricane cut right in front of him. Temporarily halting his fire, he resumed his assault from 100 yards. Right on target! As he pulled away, the Heinkel went into a vicious spiral dive, one of the crew managing to bail out. McGregor didn't wait around to confirm it, but the enemy aircraft's doom was certain.

Following in behind Red One and Two, Hartland Molson got in a quick burst at one of the bombers but with no effect. Diving away, he circled at 20,000 feet hunting for fresh prey. After several minutes he noticed a lone He 111 being chased by another Hurricane. Then, inexplicably, the British fighter discontinued his attack, probably because he was out of ammunition. Now Molson had the quarry to himself. Closing in sharply from astern to port, he let go a solid salvo that stitched the side of the Heinkel. As the bomber began to lose altitude Molson got in another shot and that did the trick. The aircraft lurched into an uncontrollable steep turn, burst into flames and smashed into the ground.

As tail-man in Yellow Section and the last to go into the attack, Arthur Yuile became separated from the rest of his mates. When a Hurricane from another squadron came into view, Yuile pulled alongside and the pair chased a formation of Heinkels heading south. But they were too far out of range. They then ran headlong into a Junkers 52 tri-motor transport-cum-bomber with distinctive blue and white stripes around the tail. Two British fighters were already attacking it from the rear, so Yuile and his newly found ally orbited while awaiting their turn. When the other three failed to bring the lumbering machine down, Yuile fired a four-second burst in the face of some sporadic return-fire, then broke left. He climbed, turned and made a quarter head-on attack from above, again without success. Now he banked around and tried again from astern, firing a five-second burst. This time his persistence paid off. Smoke billowed from a point between the fuselage and the starboard engine. Then the right undercarriage dropped down and fell away. Abandon ship! Bodies tumbled from the seemingly impregnable aircraft and parachutes quickly ballooned open. The Junkers had had it. Slowly, as if in its death throes, it rolled onto its back burping clouds of ugly black oily smoke, then dove straight to the ground, exploding near Tunbridge Wells.

After leading the attack on the German formation, Ernie McNab found himself alone at 12,000 feet near East Grinstead when he spotted a lone aircraft in the distance. At first, he made it out to be a German Jaguar, but as he got nearer he identified it as a Messerschmitt 110. McNab got in a quick shot before the twin-engine fighter dived out of sight leaving him with a damaged to his credit.

Pete Lochnan got down safely with a dead-stick landing near Romney. Tommy Little was not so lucky. Flying as Green Two, he was hit in the leg during the run at the bombers. Bailing out, he was picked up and immediately taken to hospital. Despite these setbacks, however, with a score of three enemy aircraft destroyed and two damaged, the day been an impressive one for the squadron, not to mention timely. The Brass, in the form of George Walsh, the Air Officer Commanding the RCAF Overseas, and entourage, had picked that very afternoon to pay the unit a visit.

Elsewhere, other Canadians also distinguished themselves. Andrew Fletcher, the Blenheim pilot from Lethbridge, added an Me 109 to his credit, while from North Weald Butch Barton played a major part in 249 Squadron's tally of four Heinkel 111s damaged. But the biggest shooter of the day was Winnipegger James "Smudger" Smith of 73 Squadron. Flying from an advanced field at Castle Camp, the Hurricane pilot shot down one Me 110 and damaged another. Harry Edwards, also from Winnipeg and a member of 92 Squadron, was the day's only Canadian casualty, the thirteenth to lose his life in action since the battle started.

Unsettled weather over the next few days brought some respite. On September 12, the affable Parliamentary Under-Secretary of State for Air, Harold Balfour, a WWI RFC type, arrived at Northolt to report to No. 1 Fighter Squadron RCAF on the progress of the Joint Air Training Plan at home. He candidly admitted it had initially encountered rough air, but that most of the teething problems were being overcome. The squadron's diarist could barely disguise his disgust. In words tinged with cynicism, he wrote: "It appears the Empire Scheme is plodding along in a fashion that is satisfactory to everybody, including the Germans no doubt, in that after six months travail, the scheme will produce some pilots to be sent over here in January. They may surprise everybody by sending along a handful in November who will probably be chosen reading from the bottom of the class. Considering that it takes an elephant twenty months to produce an offspring, this is considered a good show by all."

Actually, in fairness, the growth of the RCAF and the early results achieved by the British Commonwealth Air Training Plan, given the limited facilities and personnel available, were quite commendable. From the outbreak of the war in September 1939 until the end of that year, RCAF strength had doubled from just over 4,000 to 8,287. Operational forces in Canada increased to fourteen squadrons. Early in 1940, four training commands had been implemented. On April 25, the first of the seventy-four planned BCATP training schools had opened — No. 1 Initial Training School in Toronto — right on schedule to the day! By July, the first Elementary Flying Training, Service Flying Training, Air Navigation, Air Observer, and Bombing and Gunnery Schools were in operation. Recognition of these accomplishments and the country's early combat successes overseas was seen in the appointment of the country's first Minister of National Defence for Air, Charles "Chubby" Power.

In a way, No. 1 Squadron's diarist's prediction had been remarkably prescient; a handful of BCATP trainees did arrive overseas in November. But he could take solace in the fact that the thirty-seven air observers who made up the first draft of graduates to be posted to the UK were of a calibre well above the class dropouts he had feared. Fresh from No. 1 Air Navigation School at Trenton, they had all passed with honours and, after disembarking at Liverpool, were ready for operational training before going into combat.

Lunching with his military chieftains in Berlin on the day after Balfour's visit to Northolt, Hitler was in high spirits. Buoyed by reports that the nightly bombings were devastating London and assured by Goering that given a few days good weather the Luftwaffe would clear the skies of the RAF, he was still hopeful an invasion would be superfluous. But figuratively, the British weren't taking any chances. That night, Bomber Command hit the invasion ports sinking eighty troop barges.

Meanwhile, at 12 Group things were getting out of hand. Leigh-Mallory had upped the ante. He told Douglas Bader he could have two additional squadrons for his Duxford Wing. Bader was euphoric and could hardly wait to put his formation of five squadrons of sixty fighters to the test. His Canadians, among them Stan Turner, Willie McKnight, Norrie Hart, Marvin Brown, Noel Stansfeld, Laurie Cryderman, Hugh Tamblyn and the rest of 242 Squadron were as gung-ho as their CO. But when Dowding and Park learned of it, they were stunned. The impracticality of such a huge wing in the face of the need for instant backup to prevent the

German bombers from reaching their targets was horrendous. It would take seventeen minutes to get the "Balbo" — named after Marshal Italo Balbo who led large formations of Italian planes around the world — airborne and it would take up another twenty minutes before it could set course for the patrol line. Too much, too late. Here on the eve of what they knew was about to be the crucible of the battle, Leigh-Mallory was tampering with tactics, trying to further himself, the consequences of which could be highly detrimental.

On September 14, Hitler changed his mind again. Sea Lion was still "Go" but the decision on the final date it was to be launched was postponed for another three days. Meanwhile, everything depended on defeating the RAF quickly. Showers and local thunderstorms over southern England limited actions on both sides. Most of the aircraft the Luftwaffe sent over were fighters and, on Park's orders, the British fighters studiously avoided combat with them wherever possible, saving their energies for the bombers. This left an erroneous impression among German aircrews that RAF strength had been reduced to fractional proportions and that what attacks it did muster were uncoordinated or half-hearted.

That afternoon, an action by the "Caribou Squadron," the nickname assigned to No. 1 RCAF, illustrated how Fighter Command operations on that day could so easily have been misconstrued, particularly by a regimented type of mind that focussed straight ahead without any peripheral vision — as if wearing blinkers.

On patrol south of Biggin Hill, while attacking a lone Dornier 215 twin-engine bomber, the Hurricane pilots suddenly found themselves enveloped in heavy, dark cloud and became separated. As Pete Lochnan broke through the drizzling overcast, flying Green Three — his aircraft clearly identified with the squadron markings "YO" punctuated with the roundel and his own letter "N" on both sides of the fuselage — he found himself tagging along behind Blue Section. Trying to locate his own group, he spotted the sole Dornier. Two members of Blue Section quickly made a pass at it followed by Lochnan who dove down from the rear encountering no return fire. He pulled up just in time to witness a second attack by a Hurricane. Bits flew off the Dornier as Lochnan came in from the stern quarter. Then the German bomber temporarily vanished into a cloud. Seeing a break ahead, Lochnan took one last shot at it but failed to see any result. He then set course for home.

An observer, and particularly the crew of that Dornier, had they been lucky enough to survive, might understandably have been under the misapprehension that the attack by twelve Hurricanes on a single aircraft coming at it from all angles here and there, darting in and out of clouds and inflicting probably only minor damage, was hopelessly disorganized, haphazard and irresolute when, in reality, the Canadians had put up a gallant and determined effort under the most adverse and difficult weather conditions. But the misinterpretations of that day's RAF operations which reached the *Reichsmarschall* and the Fuehrer that evening, reinforced their reckoning that the day of destiny was at hand.

Instead, the overconfident Nazi leaders might have been better disposed to regard such incidents as what really lay ahead. The squadron log entry "Credited to Squadron as a whole 1 Do 215 Damaged" (later amended to give Lochnan sole honours), like the German aircrew reports told only part of the story. RCAF pilots and their RAF comrades-in-arms that Saturday had to wrestle with foul weather and restrict their attacks to bombers. Yet despite such aggravations and limitations, Fighter Command flew 860 sorties. Hugh Dowding had masterfully and wisely husbanded his resources for the showdown he knew was certain to come once the clouds blew away.

That night, although the weather had begun to clear, the Luftwaffe raids on London were unusually sparse with only fifty-five bombers over the city. It could only mean one thing. A herald. No doubt about it. On the morrow the Germans would try their damnedest to strike the major mortal blow — a dagger thrust at the very heart of RAF Fighter Command.

# CHAPTER SEVENTEEN

# RECKONING: SEPTEMBER 15

There must have been nearly a thousand aeroplanes milling in a small area just south of London. It was a quick shot away for someone was sure to be on your tail. After fifteen minutes there was hardly a plane in the sky — the Germans had run for home.

Ernie McNab, *Rockliffe Air Review*

The events of September 15th were decisive.

Hugh Halliday, *The Canadian Years*

. . . the culminating date.

Winston Churchill, *The Gathering Storm*

As the dawning sun slowly burned off the low-lying, early morning mists that had settled over southeast England that Sunday, Canadian fighter pilots — scattered over some thirty aerodromes — greeted what Keith Park characterized as "one of those days of autumn when the countryside was at its loveliest," with mixed feelings and emotions.

Wandering down to dispersal at Northolt after a solid breakfast of kippers, toast, and tea, Eric Beardmore was nursing a king-sized Mayfair hangover. As he entered the hut, he pulled on his Mae West life-jacket, plunked himself down on the nearest cot, rolled onto his side, and fell asleep.

Over at Middle Wallop, Skeets Ogilvie lounged in a deck-chair outside 609 Squadron's pilots' hut reading a paperback while basking in the growing warmth of the sun. He had no inkling he would become involved in the single most significant headline-making bombing incident of the entire day's fighting.

Deane Nesbitt of No. 1 Squadron RCAF was his usual cheery self. Before the day was out, however, it would be one he would not soon forget — albeit somewhat ruefully. His squadron mate, Ross Smither, was due to go on twenty-four hours' leave. He was looking forward to it. He needed the break. But it was destined never to be.

Up north at Coltishall, Canadian pilots were in enthusiastic spirits over the prospect of being part of a five-squadron Big Wing, despite Keith Park's and Hugh Dowding's misgivings of which they were unaware (the exception might have been their CO Douglas Bader). The day would turn out to be one of Stan Turner's more spectacular.

Likewise Ken Lawrence, sunning himself at Hornchurch, was also in for some memorable moments. But none of these participants, and this included all aircrews, Allied or German, nor their commanders or even heads of state, had any idea that the next twelve hours would decide this date as the most significant, in some ways, in European history since June 18, 1815. And like the Battle of Waterloo, the Battle of Britain would be fought on the Sabbath.

Hermann Goering, operating on the assumption that RAF Fighter Command had been reduced to a mere handful of aircraft, fixed September 15 as his final bid for air supremacy. He ordered Albert Kesselring, his chief of Luftflotte 2, to hurl in every available bomber and fighter in two titanic daylight assaults on London. Ostensibly it had the twin objectives of drawing up what was left of Fighter Command and finishing it off, as well as terrorizing the population of the world's largest metropolis into submission. But even if every bomber got through and dropped its bombs right on target, the total explosive power would be just 400 tons, hardly enough to cow a population of over ten million. Under the misguided notion that their plan would be providing maximum protection, the Germans agreed that for both attacks the Messerschmitt 109s would revert to the close-escort role that had been recently abandoned due to the fact that it limited the speed and manoeuvrability of the fighters.

Thanks to the Enigma decoding device, the British not only knew of the raid but when it was coming and that it would be in two waves. (This information was strictly classified and only Dowding and Park in Fighter Command were privy to it.) It enabled them to plan strategy and tactics in advance. Defensively this gave them an edge. But this intelligence served only to alert. Clausewitz said "war is the province of uncertainty." No manner of alarm could eradicate a potential danger. In the final analysis, the outcome depended on the pilots.

With his bomber strength cut in half by losses over the past weeks, Kesselring could not afford any diversionary manoeuvres and his shortage of fighters meant he had to time the raids so that some of the aircraft could take part in both. This ruled out any chance that the second attack could catch Park's fighters on the ground. However, he had arranged with Hugo Sperrle to divert some of Luftflotte 3's bombers from their night assignments to attack Portland during the second raid. At the same time, his own twin-engine Messerschmitt 110s would stage a bombing raid on the Supermarine factory at Eastleigh where Spitfires were coming off the line. In this way he hoped to catch Christopher Brand's 10 Group off-guard in the west while it was supporting Park's fighters in 11 Group to the east.

At approximately 10:30 a.m., the first blips appeared on the radar screens showing Luftwaffe formations building up over Calais and Boulogne. This information was relayed by telephone to 11 Group operations room at Uxbridge where Women's Auxiliary Air Force (WAAF) plotters began tracing RAF and Luftwaffe movements on a map table with coloured blocks. Prime Minister Churchill and his wife were absorbed spectators. Fifteen minutes earlier, when the PM had arrived, Park had greeted him with the non sequitur, "It's pretty quiet right now."

By this time he had already brought many squadrons to instant readiness with the pilots strapped into their aircraft ready to "press tits" on a second's notice. At 11:30 a.m., when the Germans reached the English coast, Park already had twenty-one squadrons airborne, ten of them in pairs.

Over 100 German Dornier 17 bombers and their 400 fighter escorts proceeded north to London stacked up in layers between 15,000 and 26,000 feet. Battle was not far off, and when it started Canadians proved to be everywhere. Ogilvie's 609 Squadron of Spitfires from 10 Group was on its way east to patrol the Windsor-Brooklands line. Johnny Bryson was the first among his countrymen to see action that day. His squadron, 92, based at Biggin Hill, was one of the first units in 11 Group to get off. Bryson latched onto the tail of a Junkers 88 and began firing. But he got in too close. Caught in the bomber's slipstream, he was flipped aside by the prop-wash and tumbled away.

At 11:25 a.m., 242 Squadron led by Douglas Bader had taken off from Coltishall for Duxford to form up with four other squadrons. Fifteen minutes later, twelve Hurricanes from No. 1 Squadron RCAF left Northolt to patrol over Biggin Hill aerodrome, twenty miles south of London, at 18,000 feet. After circling for half an hour, the Hurricanes were suddenly bounced by a group of Messerschmitt 109s from above and out of the sun. They broke into the attack, but for Ross Smither it was too late. One of the enemy fighters was onto his tail and his aircraft dove straight down into the ground.

Only Ernie McNab and Deane Nesbitt, who was flying number three in Red Section, got in bursts at the attackers. McNab's fire was unfruitful. But, when a 109 crossed right in front of Nesbitt, he let go a shot at close range. Before he could observe the result, however, he came under fire himself from another German fighter and, when his cockpit filled with smoke, he was forced to bail out. Alighting near Tunbridge Wells, he was picked up by members of the Home Guard and, because he was suffering from head injuries, was taken to hospital. His rescuers reported they had seen the Me 109 he had been attacking come down in flames. This was confirmed by Ernie McNab and Gordie McGregor.

Only five minutes after No. 1 RCAF Squadron came under attack, the Duxford Wing encountered the enemy over Gravesend, south of the Thames to the east of London. But unlike McNab and his band, it held the height and sun advantage. The "Canadian" squadron and two other Hurricane units were flying line-abreast at 23,000 feet with two Spitfire squadrons stepped up above at 26,000 and 27,000 feet. The German formation was well below at 17,000 feet with Me 109 fighter escorts tucked in so close to the Dorniers there was little room to manoeuvre and their speed, cut substantially to stay with the bombers, placed them at a serious disadvantage. As soon as they spotted the Germans, the Big Wing pilots, joined by four other Hurricane squadrons — a total of ninety-eight aircraft! — waded in from above. The result turned into a shambles for the enemy.

In the attack, 242 Squadron alone shot down six planes for the loss of one Hurricane whose pilot survived. Noel Stansfeld and Stan Turner each accounted for a Do 17 destroyed, while Norrie Hart sent an Me 109 down in flames. In addition, Hugh Tamblyn shared in the destruction of one of the bombers with another pilot.

The real highlight of the noon fighting that day, however, was Skeets Ogilvie's victory over a Dornier 17. Before the former bank cashier from Ottawa had tangled with it, the bomber had dropped two bombs on Buckingham Palace, the fourth time this royal domicile had been bombed. Neither of the explosives went off, though one of them damaged the Queen's private apartments. The other fell harmlessly on the lawn. Ogilvie's quarry ended up a wreck outside a pub in Pimlico much to the delight of the patrons who were lifting a pint after church. It was also a godsend to British propagandists.

Park had gambled heavily, putting most of his squadrons in the air with help from 10 and 12 Groups. But it had paid off. The Germans had gone home to lick their wounds in time to launch a second thrust. Meanwhile, with all the British fighters landing around 1:00 p.m., there was plenty of time to rearm and refuel while the pilots had lunch, in preparation for the second attack.

That raid developed at 2:00 p.m. and came in three waves, turning into a running fight all the way to London. Twenty-three squadrons from

11 Group were off the ground, five from 12 Group and three from 10 Group. Park had committed every squadron available. Watching from the control headquarters at Uxbridge, Churchill had become acutely conscious of the group commander's concern. Turning to him he asked, "What other reserves have we?" As calmly as he could Park answered, "There are none." As Churchill wrote later: "The odds were great; our margins small, the stakes infinite."

Taking off at 2:05 p.m., after patrolling for half an hour south of Biggin Hill at 20,000 feet, No. 1 Squadron RCAF intercepted a formation of some twenty-five Heinkel 111 bombers two thousand feet below escorted by Me 109 fighters. In the mêlée that ensued, the unit destroyed two of the bombers, probably destroyed three more and damaged two others. In addition, one of the pilots shared in the destruction of a Heinkel with five fighters from another squadron. The only casualty: one Canadian pilot slightly wounded.

Leading the attack, Ernie McNab got in a quick burst of fire at the nearest He 111 which dropped its bombs. Then the starboard engine started to smoke and it broke formation to take refuge in a cloud layer. McNab's own words told what happened next: "I was attacked by Me 109s. Later I saw a lone HE 111 and attacked. He dove towards clouds and two other Hurricanes attacked. He came out of clouds and I attacked again until no ammunition left. The He 111 landed on the flats of the North Shore of the estuary near Southend."

Flying number two in Blue Section, Dal Russel reported that due to heavy British anti-aircraft fire around the bombers he was unable to make a head-on attack, his favourite tactic against bombers, particularly He 111s. The Heinkel's large, unprotected glass nose gave the crew marvellous forward visibility but rendered it highly vulnerable to head-on attack. Instead, in this case, Russel dived down from the rear. However, in the process, his Hurricane stalled and he lost height. Now he approached the bomber from astern silencing the rear-gunner and damaging the starboard engine which coughed out smoke and a short flash of flame. "[I] broke off to right," he reported, "climbed and attacked again from left to right. Experienced rear gunfire and after short burst e/a did wing over and went into a tight vertical spiral, straight for the ground. I would say its remains could be found around East or South East London suburbs." They weren't. As a result, Russel could only claim a probable.

Gordie McGregor, leading Red Section, who also scored a probable, noted in his combat report that "many Me 109s above formation did not make a concerted effort to help the bombers," the exception being before McGregor started his own section's attack, when one of the 109s wounded Arthur Yuile, his tail-man, in the arm. With a remarkable display of coolness and courage, not to mention consummate flying skill, Yuile managed to fly his Hurricane back to Northolt and land without further damage.

Meanwhile, McGregor approached the enemy formation towards its left flank, closing in from the quarter beam to astern. "Range closing from approx. 350 to 200 yards there fired full burst of 18 seconds," his combat report stated. "Return fire which was intense stopped from target a/c after approx. 5 seconds." In fact, his Hurricane was hit in both wings damaging the main spar on the port side and smashing the inboard machine-gun on the starboard side. It also had a leak in the fuel tank. He, too, was lucky to get his aircraft back safely to Northolt. His target may or may not have been so fortunate. "First the port, then the starboard engine began to smoke heavily," McGregor reported, "and several pieces came off the target which lost speed and height abruptly and disappeared into cloud below." But because of the uncertainty of its fate, McGregor had to be content with a probable score.

The third probable for the squadron that afternoon went to Bob Norris who flew the number two spot in Yellow Section. First off, Norris attacked a stray Me 109, but before he could could get a shot in, it disappeared into the clouds. He then made a steep left-hand turn at over 300 miles an hour and noticed another yellow-nosed Messerschmitt below and ahead of him. "I fired from the rear-quarter beam at about 200 yards," his combat report read. "This Me 109 did a shallow left-hand turn and I turned inside and fired two more good bursts, from about 50 yards. Smoke emerged after the first burst, and flame and smoke from cockpit after the second burst. The Me 109 fell off on one wing through the clouds and when I straightened out I was almost in them myself." Norris had become so disoriented during the engagement that he had to land at nearby Biggin Hill to get his bearings.

Norris' section leader, Paul Pitcher, finished the day credited with a damaged He 111. He had stayed behind while the other two sections attacked, waiting his chances. However, his numbers two and three never received his radio transmissions so he attacked a lone Heinkel that was straggling fifty yards behind the bomber formation by himself. Pitcher approached from above and to the left, closing to dead-astern and then opened fire. Having used up all his ammunition he broke off noting that "smoke was belching from tail and starboard engine of the e/a."

Amidst all this furious fighting, Pete Lochnan added a sense of chivalry to the scenario. Lochnan got off the ground late when he found himself the only member of Green Section able to get airborne. By the time he reached the rest of the squadron on the patrol line south of Biggin Hill, he tagged onto Blue Section. When the German formation appeared,

Lochnan made a head-on attack on one of the Heinkels, firing a single burst, then attacked again from abeam and finally pulled up behind the enemy bomber. Then he opened fire at 100 yards and closed to under fifty. He then broke off ten feet over the Heinkel and saw smoke pouring from the starboard engine. Lochnan attacked twice again this time joined by three Spitfires and two other Hurricanes. Miraculously, the German pilot somehow managed to elude his assailants sufficiently to stay in the air and in one piece to make a perfect wheels-down landing at West Malling. In true courtly fashion, Lochnan landed alongside the enemy bomber, shut his engine off, climbed out of his aircraft, and helped carry the wounded German crewmen out of their plane. His knightly conduct did not deny him a victory, however. He was still awarded credit for one Heinkel destroyed. After all, even though the German bomber was far from demolished, for all his gallantry, Lochnan had rendered it, and its crew, *hors de combat.*

Simultaneously, while McNab and company were getting in their licks not far away, their Canadian cousins from Coltishall/Duxford were embroiled in a shoot-out of their own. The Big Wing had reached 18,000 feet in the area southeast of London between Kenley and Maidstone when anti-aircraft bursts signalled the position of the incoming German bombers. This time the British fighters were at a disadvantage, 4,000 feet below the enemy aircraft. Douglas Bader climbed his 242 Squadron after the bombers but just then their fighter escort pounced down on them. Now, in reversal of standard procedure, Bader ordered the Hurricanes after the fighters and the Spitfires after the bombers.

Right off the bat, Stan Turner got onto the tail of a Messerschmitt 109 and opened fire, seeing strikes around the fuselage of the enemy fighter. It went into a spin but then he lost sight of it as a section of 109s pounced on him. A cannon shell exploded near the tail of his Hurricane sending it down in a spin. As he broke through the clouds, he straightened out to find a Dornier 17 dead ahead of him. Wheeling in from the side, he gave it a deflection burst. The starboard engine belched black smoke and the bomber peeled off into a gentle dive from which it never recovered. Striking the ground between two houses, it blew apart. That victory made Turner the top scoring Canadian for the day.

Meanwhile, John Latta was eluding a 109 which overshot, placing him right on the German's tail. From fifty yards, so close it was impossible to miss, Latta only needed a five-second burst to send it flaming down out of control into a cloud bank.

Noel Stansfeld added to his earlier tally by sharing in the destruction of an He 111 with two other Hurricane pilots. He had been driven down out of formation by the Me 109s and, when he righted his aircraft at

1,000 feet and saw the other two Hurricanes chasing the 111, he joined in the hunt. Opening fire three times, he finally put one of the bomber's engines out of business. The German pilot pancaked his machine wheels-up in a field where the five-man crew were taken prisoner.

These and the members of No. 1 Squadron RCAF were not the only Canadians to post scores on this day of the Battle of Britain Day. Butch Barton, flying from North Weald with 249 Squadron, destroyed one Dornier 215 and shared in the destruction of another.

During the morning raid over London, Jimmy Cochrane of 257 — the "Burma" Squadron — spotted a Dornier 17 several thousand feet below him and dived at it, firing from the port side as another Hurricane joined him attacking from the opposite beam. Riddled by bursts from the scores of De Wilde rounds, the bomber flipped over on its back like a dead fish and then plunged downward, trailing smoke. One crew managed to jump clear, his parachute blossoming out before the aircraft exploded in a shower of fragments just above the cloud layer.

In the afternoon assault, over the Thames Estuary, the same squadron again encountered the enemy when they were bounced by yellow-nosed Me 109s. Breaking away from the attack, Cochrane joined three others in clobbering a Heinkel 111, which they forced down onto the mud flats at Foulness.

Ken Lawrence of 603 Squadron, flying a Spitfire from Hornchurch while mixing it up with Me 109 fighter-escorts, succeeded in destroying one and damaging two. This brought his string of victories to two-and-a-third destroyed, two probably destroyed, and five damaged. Another Canadian Spitfire pilot stationed at Hornchurch — with 41 Squadron — also scored that day. East of London, Casselman native, John Boyle, chalked up an Me 109 and shared in bringing down a Dornier with four others. Peter O'Brian, now CO of 152 Squadron, shared in the destruction of a Heinkel 111 bomber with two of his squadron pilots.

Two Winnipeggers also distinguished themselves in the fighting. Smudger Smith of 73 Squadron, flying a Hurricane out of Debden, destroyed an Me 109 fighter, while Spitfire pilot Allan Edy of 602 Squadron from Tangmere brought down a Dornier 17 bomber.

Total honours posted by the Canadians for the day were eleven enemy aircraft destroyed, six of them bombers, five fighters; three probably destroyed, two of them bombers, one a fighter; and four damaged of which three were bombers and one a fighter. Six pilots shared in destroying another six planes, all of them bombers, one in probably destroying a bomber and another in damaging a fighter. This was altogether an impressive tally during only two German raids and at a loss of only one pilot killed and two wounded, neither seriously.

Overall, the Luftwaffe had suffered a severe mauling from a fighter force that its aircrews had been led to believe by their commanders was kaput. They had flown 1,300 sorties, sometimes in unbalanced formations of 100 bombers escorted by 400 fighters. German fighter ace Mickey Steinhoff explained, "For demonstration purposes, everything in the way of bombers and fighters was thrown in the air." Against this force, for both main assaults, the RAF had put up nearly 400 fighters at a time.

The German fighter pilot became the scapegoat. OKL (Luftwaffe head-quarters) reported "the heavy losses are due to British fighters attacking bombers in small groups without fighter escort." OKW (Headquarters Command) underlined the point stating that "large air battles and great losses . . . [were] due to lack of fighter protection."

The crux of the situation was that RAF fighters, the exception being the Duxford Wing during the second raid, were ready and waiting. Because Park had scrambled his squadrons even before the enemy reached the English coast, the Hurricanes and Spitfires in most cases held the height advantage. Once they spotted the enemy, they tore into the formations splitting them up. The German bombers were forced to drop their loads harum-scarum all over the countryside. The fighters, restricted for the most part to close-escort, did not have the flexibility or speed to properly protect the bombers. When attacked their formations became an abattoir, lame ducks and stragglers galore.

The difference was that Dowding and Park played a defensive game. Husbanding their resources until the last minute, they bided their time until the intruders were well inland where their fighters could attack at an altitude and moment of their own choosing. Goering and Kesselring were still labouring under the Blitzkrieg syndrome — Poland, France, Belgium, Holland — whose air forces they had obliterated in a matter of days. Quick one-two punches. But over southern England, that didn't work. These were not PZL biplanes or outdated and underarmed De-woitines and Morane Saulniers they were up against. These were Hurricanes and Spitfires, wielded by two master aerial strategists and tacticians in Dowding and Park.

The one weakness in the defence armour was Trafford Leigh-Mallory's unwavering belief in, and self-serving insistence on, the use of the Big Wing. During the second raid, the Duxford Wing was late making the rendezvous with the enemy and found itself at a height disadvantage of some 4,000 feet below the German formation. Douglas Bader blamed it on the fact the wing had been scrambled too late when, in fact, it had been ordered up at the same time as the other squadrons in 11 Group. The real problem was that of forming up; it took too much time to assemble five squadrons.

The controversy over this issue, between Leigh-Mallory on the one hand and Park and Dowding on the other, had reached serious proportions, the full ramifications of which were still to be felt. Two weeks later, Park was to deliver a paper to his 11 Group station commanders on the subject, entitled "Wing Formations." In part it read:

> . . . the lack of time due to short warning of the approach of raids frequently renders it inadvisable to detail Wings of three Squadrons. Experience has shown that it takes longer to dispatch, assemble and climb to operating height than one of even two pairs of Squadrons. Frequently Wings of three Squadrons have been attacked while still climbing or forming up over the Sector aerodromes. It has been found better to have even one strong Squadron of our fighters over the enemy than a Wing climbing up below them, in which attitude they are particularly vulnerable from above. . . . There is rarely time for London sectors to get Wing formations up to their desired height before the enemy reaches important bombing targets, e.g., factories, docks, Sector aerodromes.

By sunset of this day of the battle, the country was in a state of euphoria. The British Broadcasting Corporation (BBC) evening news announced that the RAF had shot down 185 planes. Just the tonic, the fillip, the Britons needed (even if the figures were highly inflated) — particularly the beleaguered Londoners who were being blitzed nightly. After the war, the Germans from their own records, what was left of them, estimated their losses at fifty-six planes, and this was generally acknowledged as "official." That this was so blithely and bureaucratically accepted as genuine seems incredulous in the face of such proven unreliability of German claims in general like U-boat sinkings and the disguise of their own submarine losses. So far as the Battle of Britain Day is concerned, common sense would indicate that the true count lay somewhere between the BBC's number (the RAF never did issue that figure though it admitted a loss of twenty-six aircraft of which thirteen pilots survived) and that of the Luftwaffe.

Another point that brings the entire question of claims into perspective is that the RAF was fighting over its own bailiwick and their combat reports could be comfortably confirmed at least in number of aircraft destroyed (from wreckage) or crashed on English soil. What could not be determined was the number of German aircraft so badly damaged they never reached France and fell victim to the English Channel. Nor the condition of the German aircraft, particularly the bombers, that made it home and the number of dead and wounded aboard.

But even if such statistics were available, they would in no way change what the RAF had accomplished by tea-time that Sunday and what the Luftwaffe had not. The bare and basic reality of the matter is that air superiority, without which a German invasion of Great Britain was doomed to failure, had not been and never could be achieved. The German air force was in worse shape than it had been at day's outset. Merely by staying in existence and intact, the RAF had won the day — and the battle.

By day's end the Luftwaffe had become convinced that Fighter Command, far from being crippled, was getting stronger. For all its faults, the Big Wing concept of so many fighters in one spot at one time — particularly on its first interception when it was helped by four other squadrons — did much to create that impression. In actual fact, the British fighter force had been stretched to, and beyond, its limits. The following day, however, the German Naval Staff concluded that the RAF was by no means defeated and that, expecting turbulent wind conditions over the next week and with late autumn fast approaching, a landing on the English coast, which required a calm sea, would be impossible. The next day the Fuehrer ordered *Seelöwe* — Sea Lion — postponed indefinitely. This the British learned through the Enigma decoding service when it intercepted a signal from the German General Staff to the officer in charge of loading supply and troop-carrying aircraft announcing that Hitler had authorized the dismantling all the air-loading equipment.

Later, without revealing this intelligence source, Churchill cautiously advised his countrymen that a critical point had been passed. In the House of Commons he said, "Sunday's action was the most brilliant and fruitful of any fought up to date by the fighters of the Royal Air Force. . . . We may await the decision of this long air battle with sober but increasing confidence."

To the fighter pilots across southeast England, over which the day's fighting had raged — a mere one-tenth of the entire island — it was just one more evening to relax and let off steam. A rewarding day's work as their individual scores attested. But they had no way of appreciating the significance of what their efforts that day had produced; that they had in fact been making history. The laconic entry in the No. 1 Squadron RCAF dairy summed up their nonchalance neatly: "This Sunday was a day of great activity . . . "

But the most pertinent, introspective comment on the scene at the time came from a neutral source. At day's end, Raymond Lee, United States military attaché in London, wrote: "I can't for the life of me puzzle out what the Germans are up to. They have great air power and they are dissipating it in fruitless and aimless attacks all over England. They must have an exaggerated idea of the damage they are doing and the effects of their raids on public morale. . . . Just as I finish writing this, the heavy guns commence giving tongue and the little Irish maid comes in to turn down my bed. She went over to Victoria to see the plane which crashed there and is very pleased because she saw the dead German crew being extracted from the wreckage."

# CHAPTER EIGHTEEN

# CONTINUANCE

Duff weather — mist, rain and clouds — over the next two days limited German attacks to sporadic daylight forays against industrial targets east of London and fighter sweeps using bombers as bait. RAF losses were eight planes for seventeen enemy aircraft shot down. Two Canadians figured in the shooting: Peter O'Brian shared in the destruction of a Junkers 88 with two others, while John Boyle with 41 Squadron brought down a Messerschmitt 109.

On both nights the Blitz on London continued, though at this stage Goering could have more effectively deployed his bomber force at a much more profitable target: Allied shipping. Providing support for the U-boats could have helped immeasurably in the blockade to starve Britain of overseas supplies of ammunition, equipment, food and precious fuel — instead of pursuing a lost cause. But Goering steadfastly refused to admit defeat and was resolutely determined to show his Fuehrer that the Luftwaffe could overcome the RAF in the "four or five days" that had become a fixation with him. With Sea Lion in the process of winding down and the heavy losses of September 15, Luftwaffe headquarters knew there was no longer four or five days left. But it was senseless to argue with the unreasonably stubborn *Reichsmarschall*. Hitler left air operations up to him. Apart from the vengeance night raids on London, the Fuehrer had lost interest in the air war with Britain. His thoughts and ambitions had turned elsewhere.

In the misguided hope that somehow RAF Fighter Command might still be worn down by a combination of bombing and air combat, Goering now directed Kesselring to supplement the night raids on London with "harassing attacks" in daylight. At the same time he also commanded increased attempts to destroy aircraft factories. He seemed curiously incapable of coming to grips with the realization that the drain on his resources on September 15 had left the Luftwaffe without enough bombers to go around for such undertakings. September 18 saw the first daylight raid on London since the 15th, for which Kesselring had to make do with minimum bomber strength. It proved a bumper date for Canadians, though. Six of the Dominion's sons contributed in the shooting down seven bombers, damaging three, and probably destroying a fighter.

At 9:24 in the morning, No. 1 Squadron RCAF was scrambled from Northolt, Gordie McGregor leading. The German aircraft, mainly fighters, had crossed the coast between North Foreland and Folkestone, and were intercepted over Maidstone and the Thames Estuary. McGregor's Hurricanes had climbed to 27,000 feet above the Estuary. In the fracas, Eric Beardmore became detached from his section and joined up with 229 Squadron. Forced to take to his parachute, he landed in the Thames near the shore. Suffering slight injuries, he was packed off to the hospital at Taplow where he joined Deane Nesbitt who was still nursing head wounds from being shot down three days earlier.

Meanwhile Otto Peterson, leading the section from which Beardmore had become separated, was on a roll. When he and his wingman were jumped by four Me 109s, they broke into the attack but were unable to get within firing range. Peterson began climbing into the sun. Suddenly, over Gravesend, he spotted three more 109s in loose formation 2,000 feet below him. With the sun at his back he began to dive, drawing a bead on the number three man, tail-end Charlie. From 300 yards he opened fire. The enemy fighter burped out some white smoke and went into a vertical dive. The other two Germans broke away downwards, one to the left the other to the right. Peterson followed the one diving to port, got in a good long burst and saw a large piece of fabric fall off its left wing. But he had to break off because an Me 109 was on his tail. Shaking it loose, he saw his second target begin a gentle dive streaming white smoke. By this time he came under attack again and was forced to pull into a steep turn to get away. By then he had lost sight of the two aircraft he had fired on. Peterson was credited with one aircraft destroyed and one damaged.

The Duxford Wing was scrambled late in the afternoon. The pilots were able to form up and position themselves at the patrol line south of London before the enemy reached it. They were waiting at 19,000 feet when anti-aircraft bursts drew their attention to the German formation 3,000 feet below and ahead of them. There were two groups of about thirty bombers each.

Flying as Douglas Bader's wingman, Willie McKnight opened fire on the Junkers 88 nearest to him setting the starboard engine on fire, where-

*Johnny Kent of Winnipeg who
single-handedly took on forty
Messerschmitts in the most
spectacular dogfight of WW II.*
(Imperial War Museum/Courtesy
John Grodzinski)

*Gordie McGregor, the oldest
pilot to fight in the Battle of
Britain. He later became
Canada's top airline executive.*
(PL 5863)

*Deane Nesbitt of Montreal. He was shot down twice and survived to head up a fighter wing. Later as one of the country's leading financiers, he handled the Trans-Canada Pipelines underwriting.* (A. D. Nesbitt Collection)

*Hartland Molson, one of the first Canadians to be shot down, became RCAF Director of Personnel. He was later called to the Senate of Canada.* (PL 8363)

*Dal Russell of Toronto. He was one of the first pilots in the Battle of Britain to win the DFC. He led two successive fighter wings.*
(PL 19373)

*Willie McKnight, Edmonton sharp-shooter, became the leading Canadian ace in the Battle of Britain.*
(Courtesy John Grodzinski)

*Pilots of 242 Squadron,
RAF, with their CO, Douglas
Bader (c.): 2nd, 3rd, 4th and
5th from left: Hugh Tamblyn,
Stan Turner, Neil Campbell,
Willie McKnight (beside Bader).
Extreme right: Marvin Brown.*
(Courtesy John Grodzinski)

*Ernie McNab, CO of No. 1
Squadron RCAF. He was the
first Canadian to win a war
medal (DFC), the second to
shoot down an enemy plane,
and the first to lead an RCAF
unit into combat.*
(PL 905)

*Stan Turner with the Allies' top ace, Johnnie Johnson. Known as "The Bull" for his bellicose manner, he ended the war with an incredible 1,125 hours and 35 minutes of combat time.*
(PL 43239)

*Neil Campbell of St. Thomas, Ont., flew with Bader's controversial Big Wing. He accounted for two enemy planes destroyed and another pair damaged before being killed in action two weeks before the Battle of Britain ended.*
(Courtesy John Grodzinski)

*Noel Stansfeld, former
stockbroker from Vancouver,
B.C. He enlisted in the RAF
before the outbreak of WW II.
He was wounded in the
Battle of Britain, and was
awarded the DFC.*
(Courtesy John Grodzinski)

*Hugh Tamblyn flew both
Defiants and Hurricanes in
the Battle. He shot down four
and a half enemy planes,
probably destroyed one, and
damaged another to earn the
DFC.*
(Courtesy John Grodzinski)

*Billy Bishop, V.C., (Air Marshal) chats with CO Ernie McNab on a visit to No. 1 Squadron RCAF during the Battle of Britain. Note McNab's polka-dot kerchief in defiance of official regulations.*
(Courtesy the Author)

*Members of No. 1 Squadron RCAF: (l. to r.): George Hyde, Bev Christmas, Vaughan Corbett, Eric Beardmore, Bob Edwards, Ed Reyno.*
(Courtesy the Author)

*Hurricane of 242 Squadron*
(Courtesy DND)

*The
Battle of Britain
Lace Tapestry*

—

*On Display
in the
Bishop Building
Air Command
Headquarters
Westwin, Manitoba*

—

*In Commemoration
of*
**THE FEW**

—

The Canadian copy of the tapestry is one of twelve out of an original thirty-eight commissioned and produced between 1942 and 1946 by the Nottingham firm of Dobsons M. and Browne and Co. Ltd., then Europe's largest lace manufacturer.

Purportedly one copy had been presented to the Canadian government and another was placed on loan. No record or trace of either could be found. Thanks to the efforts of Dick Malott, curator of the Canadian War Museum, a copy was finally acquired and placed on loan with the Air Force Heritage Fund.

Nearly fifteen feet high and five and a half feet wide, it contains a total of 26 thousand miles of the finest Egyptian cotton. Production required 4,200 threads and the preparation of 975 bobbins in the loom. The intricate design took over two years to complete.

upon the crew bailed out. Then, in company with a Spitfire, he attacked another Ju 88. Between the two they knocked out both engines. This crew also took to their parachutes, their abandoned bomber crashing into a field.

Bader's other wingman, Neil Campbell, had a field day. Although he overshot his first target, he soon had another in his sights — a lone, straggling 88. From astern he gave it a short burst, sending it tumbling down with both engines burning. He then found himself on the right-hand side of several bombers banking towards him. He opened fire on the leader but without effect. He then sighted on a second 88 which had already been mauled by a Spitfire. Like his first conquest, he sent it down in flames too, both engines afire. But he wasn't through yet. Overtaking another Junkers, he damaged its starboard engine. But the Ju's rear-gunner found his mark and Campbell's Hurricane sustained a hit in the port wing. He broke off, but quickly teamed up with a Spitfire, and between them they downed another 88 by setting both of its engines on fire.

Campbell was definitely the Canadian star of the show that afternoon. He had destroyed one Ju 88, damaged another and shared in the destruction of two others to add to his score of the Dornier he had destroyed on Battle of Britain Day.

Hugh Tamblyn had dived into the middle of the formation and found himself caught in a vicious crossfire, a highly uncomfortable — not to mention dangerous — situation. He hastily extricated himself, but not before he got in a quick burst at the handiest target. McKnight later confirmed that Tamblyn had scored a Ju 88 flamer.

Norrie Hart also scored — a pair of flamers. Singling out one of the 88s, he concentrated his aim on the cockpit. The aircraft caught fire and dived away. Hart followed it down and saw it crash near a railroad station. Pulling back up, he suddenly spotted another Junkers flying low on one engine, one of the propellers feathered. Climbing vertically below the bomber's belly, he let go a steady burst, setting the other engine on fire. That 88 crashed into the ground as well.

Another Canadian winner that day was Butch Barton, one of the first two Canadians to fly a Spitfire, though on this occasion, he made his score in a Hurricane when he damaged a Heinkel 111.

*         *         *

Back at Northolt, after a good day's outing and also having sustained an enemy air raid on the aerodrome, No. 1 Squadron RCAF was rewarded with a heavy-handed helping of red tape from its own headquarters in

London. "Scarves and sweaters will not be tolerated in future in place of collars and ties," the official directive read. Just the sort of thoughtful and considerate kind of encouragement fighter pilots in the heat of combat needed. A generous serving of good old-fashioned, unadulterated brass-hat bull. Ernie McNab had already decided on a flight path that would in effect say "Shove it!" Meanwhile, as the squadron diarist noted with unveiled cynicism, "Apparently when called from 30 minutes available to immediate readiness and expected to be airborne in no time at all, the pilots have to be inspected and passed as neat and tidy to go up and engage the King's enemies."

*        *        *

The Battle of Britain may have been won, but it was still far from over as the last two weeks of the month well illustrated. Although Goering's hopes of annihilating the RAF were gone, he at least was keeping the pot boiling. However, for the next two days there was little activity on the part of the Germans.

On September 21, Allan Edy and six other pilots from Tangmere chased a Junkers 88 along the south English coast. But far from being overwhelmed, the wily twin-engine pilot gave the Spitfires a run for their money. Although strikes were seen on the German bomber, by twisting, turning and cork-screwing the pilot managed to elude his attackers and escape across the Channel. The seven somewhat disgruntled RAF pilots had to be content with carving up a damaged among themselves.

That same day, the three Northolt squadrons — No. 1 RCAF, Johnny Kent's Polish 303, and 229 — carried out their first flight as a Wing. In a way it was as if Park had wanted to make his point. The exercise proved to be a complete balls-up. No one seemed certain who was leading so they just proceeded as vectored in a gaggle. It was probably lucky they never made an interception although "bogies" were sighted off the coast. Later Park issued his critique — about and called *Wing Formations* — to his station commanders.

Two days later, Johnny Kent destroyed a Messerschmitt 109 and a Focke-Wulf 58 in one of his most memorable encounters, one that took place mid-morning. At 23,000 feet on the far side of the Isle of Sheppey, the squadron was vectored south by the Group controller where the pilots could see white contrails at 30,000 feet — too far out of reach.

"I continued on course," Kent said later, "and was told to look out for Bandits to starboard. I turned around and saw the enemy aircraft at 25,000 feet in front — a good twenty to thirty of them somewhat scattered." These 109s were wheeling around, feinting attacks on the Hurricanes.

Kent pulled his squadron into a circle. Then the German fighters broke off and made more fake passes at different angles, but from a distance too far away to fire. After orbiting for several minutes, two of them came at the Poles head on. Kent turned slightly to the right and the German planes followed suit. In the next moment an Me 109 cut in front of him at right angles. From 400 yards he let go a full deflection shot. "The enemy went into a steep dive towards the coast," Kent said. "I allowed a lot of deflection and fired a short burst. I followed and, when the 109 pulled out at 4,000 feet, I got on its tail and fired a short burst at 150 yards. I fired another burst, and the smoke became so thick I could barely see it. For a moment I thought it was on fire."

Kent pulled aside and watched as the smoke gradually diminished until it was reduced to a thin white stream. By then the two planes were over the English coast and Kent attacked again, firing a burst from 100 yards. This time the Messerschmitt gave off more smoke but continued on a straight course. Kent followed the German aircraft out to sea letting off several short squirts at close range, shooting off one of the tail struts. Part of the tail plane and a section of the cockpit canopy broke off immediately. Still the pilot took no evasive action and continued to fly in a straight line. Kent climbed up to one side and started a quarter-beam attack. But before he could open fire, the Messerschmitt rolled over on its back and the pilot bailed out. As the enemy flyer floated down in his parachute about mid-Channel, Kent turned for home.

Approaching the coast, he sighted a twin-engine aircraft flying low over the water. It was like no plane he'd ever seen before. Because he couldn't distinguish it from friend or foe, he drew up close to have a better look. "It had dappled grey colouring," he reported, "and black crosses on the wings and fuselage." Foe! Kent opened fire and saw his De Wilde bullets rake the aircraft from stem to stern, yet it still remained airborne. "The rear-gunner did not open fire," Kent added. "I think my first burst must have disabled him; but as my engine was running rough and my ammunition was practically exhausted, I broke off and returned to base."

From his description the aircraft was identified by intelligence as a Focke-Wulf 58, an aircraft rarely seen in the Battle of Britain or at anytime or anywhere else. Kent was given credit for damaging it.

For the past few days the bombers had done little damage in the daytime although at night they were turning London into what the British press described as "Dante's Inferno." On the afternoon of September 24, however, twenty Me 109 fighter-bombers struck hard at the Supermarine factory at Woolston, near Southampton, in broad daylight. Though little harm was done to the Spitfire plant itself, explosives landed in the air-raid shelter killing nearly 100 workers.

That day and the next were signal ones for the "Palace Protector" — Skeets Ogilvie of 609 Squadron. On September 24, he tangled with a Dornier 17 and probably destroyed it. That brought his total victories to two aircraft destroyed and two probably shot down. Next day he added another probable to his list — a Do 17 again — along with a damaged Me 110. This was indeed good news in the face of the loss of Johnny Bryson who was killed the day before while flying a Spitfire with 92 Squadron which was based at Biggin Hill.

Before lunch that day (September 23), Canadians of No. 1 Squadron RCAF and Poles of 303 Squadron joined forces to fly two wing patrols, both of them uneventful. But the afternoon told a different story.

At 2:30 p.m., Otto Peterson, with Dal Russell as his wingman, were dispatched to investigate a reported single-engine Bogie flying towards the English coast near the Isle of Wight. Twenty minutes later the pair had climbed to 14,000 feet and were twelve miles north of Tangmere, when Russel spotted a stray aircraft below them flying an irregular pattern as if, in his own words, "it was looking for something." He immediately radioed his sighting to Peterson. As they got closer they recognized it as a twin-engine Dornier 215.

Peterson dove at the German bomber in a sweeping quarter-beam head-on attack. He was followed closely by Russel. Too close! As Peterson opened fire, Russel's Hurricane was showered with empty cartridge cases flying back from the underwing ammunition waste ducts of Peterson's fighter. It so blurred his vision he couldn't take aim. And Peterson encountered such heavy return fire from the Dornier's nose-gunner that he had to break off.

Now Russel led the attack, coming in from astern on the enemy plane and "gave him all [he] had," expending every last bit of his ammunition. Peterson watched his wingmate's tracers "definitely going into the e/a." This time there was no return fire and Peterson, who had also run out of ammunition, broke off his second attack from between 150 and 200 yards away. By this time the Dornier had keeled over in a steep dive to starboard and disappeared into the clouds below. Although Peterson reported that he believed "one of the engines was stopped," its fate remained unknown to the Hurricane pilots until they landed back at Northolt at 3:10. They were met with the welcome news that the Observer Corps had confirmed they had seen the German bomber fall into the sea near Worthington. Peterson and Russel were each credited with sharing a destroyed.

They and the rest of the squadron were also greeted with a visit by my father, Billy Bishop, V.C., who was by then wearing the stripes of an Air Marshal. He was in Britain on a public relations tour as part of his job as chief of recruiting for the RCAF. He was accompanied by the Air Officer Commanding the RCAF overseas, George Walsh. As the squadron diarist duly noted, "The movie camera people had a field day." Not only the newsreels but the press too. The opportunity to publicly snub the spit-and-polish directive from headquarters a week earlier was not lost on Ernie McNab. Much to my father's amusement, the squadron CO used the occasion to sport a blue kerchief with white polka-dots around his neck. And that's exactly what appeared — not only on the screen and in the papers and magazines, but in the official records as well.*

*            *            *

*At least McNab was wearing the ring in his hat that kept it firm in pukka-parade form. Later, RCAF officers discarded the ring almost from the moment they embarked from Canada for overseas. This gave the hats a fashionable floppy, cavalier look. How or when or by whom this started is anyone's guess.

However, I am reasonably sure of at least one source concerning another form of fighter-pilot swank: the top button left undone on the tunic. In 1917, after my father had been awarded the Victoria Cross and had reached the status of top British ace, he was photographed beside his Nieuport fighter. Close inspection shows he had left his top button undone. It was probably accidental. The Royal Flying Corps in France in World War I wasn't much on ceremony or formality insofar as dress code goes. At the time that picture was taken, it received worldwide circulation. It was also extensively used for propaganda purposes when WWII began. It is just possible it triggered the idea of leaving the top button undone. Sporty.

In terms of fighter-pilot dress, things changed rather dramatically in the years following the Battle of Britain. In my day, three years afterwards, although we dressed formally for dinner in the Officers Mess, I flew my entire tour with only a school hockey sweater under my battle-dress jacket and a white scarf around my neck — with almost official blessing. Contrary to the order about collars and ties in B of B days, we were strongly advised against wearing them. And for a very simple reason. If you had to parachute into the water and were wounded, a wet tie could shrink and strangle you.

In closing this digression, I must add that certain superstitions went with the flamboyance of wearing scarves. You were warned by squadron mates not to wash them no matter how soiled they got. Accepted superstition dictated that washing them was an open invitation to getting shot down. I ignored this advice because my neckwear had become so filthy. The result? Exactly what I had been warned against happened. But I did crash-land with the cleanest white scarf in all of Normandy.

Most members of No. 1 RCAF avoided spending their evenings in London. As their official diarist reported on one instance: "London got another pasting according to the leave boys, who thought the rain might cause hostilities to cease and mistakenly spent the night in town. They are now completely cured."

Not so for Hartland Molson. Although he had been flying two or three hours that day and knew there was no let-up in the nightly blitz on London, because he was one of my father's closest friends he accepted his invitation that evening to go into "Danté's Inferno" to join him for dinner at Claridge's Hotel. After their meal they took the "lift" to the top floor and climbed a short stairway to the roof where my father had arranged for chairs, ice and whisky — all the comforts for a ringside seat from which they could watch the bombing through binoculars.

It amounted to a question of who was the safest — Molson or his buddies back at Northolt? While Molson had been in the middle of one raid, he'd missed another. In his absence the aerodrome had been bombed. Two barracks were hit; fortunately, there were no casualties.

Next afternoon, King George VI visited the RCAF squadron, a slightly more formal occasion than the one on the day previous. In deference to royal protocol, Ernie McNab's scarf was noticeably missing as the pilots lined up to shake hands with His Majesty who, the squadron diarist noted, "Congratulated the squadron on its work and took a keen interest in the proceedings." The same scribe had harsher words for another VIP visitor to Northolt that day. Viscount Gort [who had been in charge of the Dunkirk evacuation] "was also on the station this morning," he wrote. "The CO had a chatter with him and was not particularly impressed."

Though there was "no joy" for the RCAF in battle during the day, other Canadians added to their scores. Skeets Ogilvie damaged a Heinkel 111, while Alan Edy of 601 Squadron brought his Spitfire's guns to bear on a Heinkel as well, and was cited as having scored a probable. This took place during another raid on the Supermarine factory at Woolston, this time by seventy-six German bombers. Three Spitfires on the production line were trashed and others were damaged. But the latter were soon repaired and ready for delivery to the squadrons. Beaverbrook's energetic program, despite enemy interference, was maintaining a steady flow of fighters off the assembly lines. On average, 150 Spitfires were being completed every month. To minimize the risk, a shadow factory had been set up at Castle Bromwich in the Midlands. As well, the Southampton facilities had been extended to more than thirty-five different sites. Industrious Canadian ingenuity at work.

# CHAPTER NINETEEN

# "THE THIRD GREAT AND GLORIOUS DAY"

## Friday, September 27

**Activity:** Heavy daylight attacks on London and Bristol. By night incursions against London, Merseyside and the Midlands.

**Weather:** Fair in the extreme south and southwest. Cloudy over the Channel with haze.

**Score/** Fifty-five German aircraft listed as missing (twenty-one of them
*Overall:* bombers). Twenty-eight Allied planes lost (most of which came down on land).

*Canadian:* Twelve enemy aircraft destroyed, two probably destroyed, and eight damaged.

Churchill called it "the third great and glorious day of the Fighter Command during the course of the Battle of Britain." It also marked the last of the massive daylight assaults by big bomber formations on London. And, not since Battle of Britain Day twelve days earlier, had Canadian fighter pilots experienced such combat.

The first sign of Luftwaffe activity appeared on the plotting table at 11 Group operations headquarters in Uxbridge shortly after eight o'clock in the morning. A mixed bag of bomb-carrying Messerschmitt 110s, Junkers 88, Dornier 215 and Heinkel 111 bombers, escorted by Me 109 and 110 fighters, stepped up between 14,000 and 20,000 feet. From Enigma-deciphered intelligence, Commander Park had learned that the target was London and he positioned his fighters in relays all along the route, starting at Dungeness on the coast, to harass the enemy formations all the way to the capital. And No. 1 Squadron RCAF was right in the thick of it.

Scrambled from Northolt along with 303 Squadron, both units were ordered to attack the bombers in the vicinity of Kenley. Twenty-five minutes later at 18,000 feet, they spotted a gaggle of Ju 88s escorted by the single-engine Me 109 and twin-engine Me 110 fighters. The bombers were flying in stepped-down sections of three.

As Caribou leader in charge of both squadrons, Ernie McNab led the attack against the bombers with the two members of his section — Bev Christmas and Edward de Peyster Brown, an American from Coronado, California — in tow. As they dove, the enemy aircraft turned heel, forcing the Hurricanes to close in from astern. Picking out the left-hand Junkers in the rear section, all three opened fire whereupon the German pilot dropped his bombs and turned south heading pell-mell for the coast, the Hurricanes giving chase, firing as they closed in. Suddenly, two of the crew jumped from the aircraft. One parachute opened and, although it was badly tattered, it ballooned sufficiently to carry its occupant to safety. The other crew dropped his parachute and fell to his death. But the Junkers continued its flight. McNab pulled up close and gave it a quick two-second burst that finished it off. It plummeted nose-first and exploded in flames in the village of Limpsfield. The three pilots shared the victory between them. . . .

Meanwhile, other members of McNab's squadron had been busy. Dal Russel, flying number three in Otto Peterson's Green Section, was attacked by an Me 109 from behind. Taking evasive action by turning sharply to face his assailant, he found himself on the tail of three Messerschmitts flying in line-astern. From seventy yards, directly behind and underneath, he gave the hindmost German aircraft a three-second burst. Russel was unable to determine what damage he had inflicted, but the 109 fell out of formation and the pilot bailed out. The aircraft crashed in a field behind a large house near a small town.

As Russel broke away he lost height but, searching about, he saw Ernie McNab who also had found himself alone after his section shot down the Ju 88. Now the two teamed up and climbed back to 18,000 feet where twenty Me 110s had gone into a defensive circle over Biggin Hill. As the two Canadians drew near, one of the Messerschmitts broke from the circle and headed south for the coast. Russel and McNab closed in behind it. However, in the attack, they became separated.

Still following the Me 110, McNab was joined by another Hurricane which emerged out of nowhere. McNab gave the enemy fighter a squirt and saw an explosion and flames along the port side; then the aircraft turned on its back and smashed into the ground near Crowborough.

While this was taking place, Russel single-handedly attacked a covey of 110s. Picking out one of them, he curved in behind it in a tight turn. Ten seconds of fire from his eight Browning machine-guns was all he needed to set its port engine on fire. Four other Hurricanes now pounced on the hapless fighter and sent it crashing into a field north of East Grinstead. Then another Me 110 loomed ahead and the Hurricanes set upon it. In a matter of minutes it too spun earthwards, just south of where Russel's first victim had fallen.

Bob Norris, Paul Pitcher's number two for this outing, got into the act when he damaged one of the Me 110s. "We got Tally Ho and went into V formation," his combat report read. "We carried out an attack on an He 111. Seeing that it was already crippled, our section broke away. I turned in the van and lost my section momentarily, then noticed an enemy twin-engine with our aircraft attacking it. I made a front-quarter attack from below and closed to short range. I noticed bits fly off it and smoke pour out of the port engine. The Me 110 began losing altitude and I broke off as it was well escorted by fighters."

Pete Lochnan's Hurricane was hit by cannon and machine-gun fire while making a pass at an Me 109. Half of his right aileron was shot off, so he started back to base. Enroute he saw a Ju 88 being attacked by a Hurricane. Since his damaged aircraft was still airworthy, he decided to join in. He got in one burst but held back when three other Hurricanes bounced it, sending it crashing into a house. Lochnan now climbed for home but saw a 110 under fire from one of the pilots from 303 Squadron and hastened to help. He got in three good bursts of his own, one from a rear climbing angle, another from the port-quarter, after which smoke spewed from the enemy aircraft. Then one of the other Hurricanes struck it from the starboard side. By this time the fight had brought them down to 500 feet. But the Messerschmitt pilot still seemed full of spunk. Suddenly he turned to face Lochnan head-on, then just as quickly veered away and dove smack-bang into Gatwick aerodrome. Moments later Lochnan landed on the same field, his engine about to pack up. He left the Hurricane to be repaired and hitched a ride back to Northolt in a Magister touring plane.

Gordie McGregor got the better of a Ju 88 but failed to see it crash, so he only claimed a probable. But it was a victory nonetheless, although it took thirty-three years to confirm it, as we shall later learn.

All in all a good morning for the RCAF, but not without its losses. Otto Peterson went missing, and shortly afterwards it was learned he had been killed in the morning's fighting. With a score of one-and-a-half aircraft destroyed, one probable, and three damaged before he lost his life, Peterson had made a fine account of himself and had served his squadron nobly.

Other Canadians who figured in the scoring were John Milne from

Corklin, Sask., a Spitfire pilot with 605 Squadron at Kenley wounded five days earlier, who clobbered an Me 110; and Butch Barton, who also demolished a 110.

Having failed to clear the skies with fighters, and after a fearful mauling sustained over London in which the Messerschmitts were forced to make a ground-level retreat, Luftflotte 2 commander Albert Kesselring launched a split attack at 11:30 a.m., sending eighty aircraft to Bristol and 300 to London.

Three sections from No. 1 Squadron RCAF in combination with 229 Squadron were off the ground at 11:48 a.m. to patrol the Gatwick area, with Gordie McGregor leading. At half-past noon, from 18,000 feet, they spotted Me 109s above them flying in sections of line-astern. Three of the Germans dove to attack the leading section. Paul Pitcher and Arthur Yuile broke left and right respectively. One of the 109s closing in on Yuile shot past McGregor on his port side. McGregor turned sharp left, got in a burst, then banked right and fired again. The Messerschmitt spewed smoke and spun down, and McGregor was rewarded with a damaged.

At the same time, to the southeast in the Dover-Canterbury area known as "Hell's Corner," the Duxford Wing tangled with twenty Me 109s, Canadians much in evidence. At 23,000 feet with the sun at their backs and a thin layer of cloud shielding them from surprise by the higher-flying German fighters, the five squadrons held all the cards.

The most successful Canadian in this fracas was John Latta, who destroyed two Messerschmitts. Pouncing on the tail of one of them which began pulling into a steep turn, he fired a three-second burst from 150 yards. His bullets hit the fuel tank and the cockpit erupted in a mass of flames as the aircraft flipped over into a vertical dive. Latta then chased several 109s making for the coast. With a height advantage he easily overtook them and fired his first shot at the rearmost one from 250 yards. No result. Closing to 150 yards he opened fire again. This time his bullets found the mark and again it was the enemy's fuel tank. This aircraft, too, burst into flames and keeled over into the Channel.

In the heat and excitement of battle, what Latta never realized is that he had given the enemy fighter pilots plenty of target practice of their own, as his combat report later revealed: "My machine sustained damage to the tail and one wing through machine-gun fire but I did not notice this when [the] attack took place, but I imagine it was when attacking my first section. Enemy's idea of evasive tactics very poor: steep climbs and turns only ones noted. Saw three other machines go down evidently out of control but could not confirm whether ours or theirs."

At the start of the combat, Hugh Tamblyn was bounced by a 109 and dove to shake the enemy plane off his tail. Having succeeded he next proceeded to fly in the direction of a group of flak bursts that fingered another Messerschmitt, this one fleeing in the direction of France. As Tamblyn closed in from behind, the German pilot frantically started to weave to make his aim difficult. Nevertheless, Tamblyn snapped off a series of bursts that caused a stream of fuel and radiator coolant to gush from the 109. But just then Tamblyn had to break off; all his ammunition was gone and he had to reconcile himself with a damaged for his pains.

Noel Stansfeld had to settle for a probable after an even more frustrating bout. He had chased an Me 109 over Dover; then, as the German fighter fled across the Channel, it disappeared in the haze. At that moment a Ju 88 crossed his sights and straightened out right in front of him. Stansfeld let go a volley from 600 feet away. Then, as he drew within fifty feet to finish it off, the German bomber began to emit smoke and Stansfeld got ready to shoot again. But the only response to pressing the gun button was a his of air from the pneumatic feed. His ammunition had run out. "Damn it!" he noted in his combat report in which he stated that due to poor visibility he was unable to confirm whether the enemy aircraft had crashed. But he hastened to add, "I am convinced it had no chance of getting back across the Channel."

Over in 10 Group to the west where the Germans were raiding Bristol, Skeets Ogilvie got in the fray defending the Channel port with his Spitfire by shooting down an Me 110 to bring his total number of aircraft destroyed to three. (He also boasted three probables and two damaged as well.) And the Canadians were still far from through for the day.

Just before three o'clock that afternoon, with Gordie McGregor leading for the second time that day, six Hurricanes set off from Northholt with orders to patrol a line running north of Kenley to help stop a third raid on London. Once airborne, they orbited over base to give 303 Squadron, led by Johnny Kent, time to get off and rendezvous with them. And then they were joined by the other squadron on the field, 229.

By this time they could see a formation of Dornier 215 bombers well above them and they climbed as fast as they could to attack. But six of the bombers were in no mood for a fight and immediately they saw the Hurricanes they turned south and started a shallow dive towards the coast.

By the time the Hurricanes had reached 7,000 feet, they saw several small sections of Dorniers numbering about twelve each, 8,000 feet above them. Once the Hurricanes got to 15,000 feet over Croyden they waded in, every man for himself.

After the initial pass, Dal Russel, flying the number two slot in Blue

Section, lost considerable height and had to climb back up again. But the bombers had turned heel and headed south. Russel chased one of them all the way to the coast, down to 3,000 feet until he reached a point 500 yards behind the bomber. He opened fire. The Dornier reared up, then settled back down. At this precise moment Russel had to stop shooting because another Hurricane cut in front of him. The bomber flew out of sight, smoking badly, with two other Hurricanes in pursuit.

When Arthur Yuile, who flew the tail-end Charlie position in Blue Section, attacked in line-astern, he suddenly looked up to see a Do 215 about 100 feet above him. He pulled up sharply and made a full three-second deflection shot, closing to fifty yards. He then delivered a second burst to another bomber to the left of his original target. The first Dornier pulled up rigorously then fell into a violent wing-over. At this point Yuile's Hurricane stalled and, because several Me 109s were now prancing around, he dove away to port. He was unable to see what happened to his victim. Both German aircraft were probably pretty badly damaged; at the end of his combat report, Yuile wrote: "I experienced no apparent fire from the Dorniers."

Paul Pitcher attacked one of the German bombers from the left at a quarter-angle from behind the target. "After several seconds of fire from astern he pulled up steeply," Pitcher reported, "and smoke was issuing from [his] engine. I broke off and made a beam deflection shot on another [aircraft] from starboard with no visible effect and finally one attack on the same aircraft from astern above when [my] ammunition ran out."

de Peyster Brown had to return to the aerodrome on take-off because his wheels wouldn't come up, but he climbed into another Hurricane and managed to catch up with the rest of the squadron in time to see German bombers to his left and ahead top the right. (Brown was lucky to be able to take off at all. That was the last serviceable Hurricane the squadron had available, giving some idea of the limit to which aircraft resources had been stretched). As he manoeuvred into his proper position in Blue Section, he eyed a Dornier below and ahead of him being attacked by a Hurricane which suddenly broke away. Apparently the Dornier had suffered little damage because when he attacked it Brown experienced severe return fire. In spite of this, his own shooting blasted pieces off the bomber and one of the engines started to spew smoke. As Brown broke off and climbed to make a second run, the enemy aircraft burst into flames and dove straight into the ground five miles east of Tunbridge Wells. On the same patrol, McGregor damaged a Do 215.

Johnny Kent had picked out a Dornier among a formation of seven fleeing in a dive to the coast. When Kent reached a position 100 yards behind it, the rear-gunner fired and hit the Hurricane's propeller. With his own fire Kent silenced the gunner and knocked pieces off the rear of the aircraft. Then he fired a long burst into the starboard engine from seventy-five yards and the motor stopped. Now the enemy bomber began to dive even more steeply and Kent hit the other engine which began, in his own words, "to smoke fiercely." By this time, they were over the Channel and because Kent sensed the Dornier was done for anyway, he climbed up and made S-turns above it to survey the damage. His guess had been right. It was pockmarked with holes. It hit the water, skipped along the surface, then sank. As he pulled away Kent noticed a rubber dinghy surface in the spot where the bomber went under, but it appeared empty. Small wonder. During the encounter he had used up a total of 2,340 De Wilde bullets.

In the meantime, Victoria-born George Corbett, a Spitfire pilot with 66 Squadron at Kenley, got into a tangle with a Ju 88 which he shot down. But he had to make a forced landing after being hit by his own anti-aircraft fire.

He had first attacked a Do 215, and as the port engine of the bomber began to pour smoke he broke away. Climbing up for a second pass, he saw the Junkers off to his right. He dove to within fifty yards dead-astern and fired a five-second squirt. "The port engine smoked badly," he reported, "then burst into flame and threw so much smoke back that I had to break to port because of being very close and not able to see."

Then a burst of flak below and behind him shattered one elevator. Shrapnel pierced the starboard wing and the rear of the fuselage partially jamming the rudder. However, Corbett was able to navigate his stricken aircraft safely onto a nearby field. Two policemen who had watched the action confirmed that the Junkers had exploded after hitting the ground near Cockerhurst.

That was the last combat for the Canadians on September 27, all of whom were back down on the ground shortly after four o'clock in time for tea. They had plenty of reason to be proud, but three among them had cause for special celebration that evening. The awards of a DFC to Stan Turner and Noel Stansfeld, and a Bar to the same decoration for Willie McKnight, all of 242 "Canadian" Squadron, were announced. A fitting finale to a victorious day.

# CHAPTER TWENTY

# EXHAUSTION

Several days after his visit to Northolt, over lunch at Buck's Club in Mayfair with the Parliamentary Under-Secretary for Air, Harold Balfour, my father commented: "Our fellows are getting pretty tired." Balfour nodded in agreement. "I know," he replied. "They all are. But I'm afraid they'll have to stick it out a bit longer." No. 1 Squadron RCAF medical officer, John Nodwell, complained to his superiors that the pilots had not had any leave since arriving in England in June. He added: "There is a definite air of constant tension and they are unable to relax as they are practically on constant call. The pilots go to work with forced enthusiasm and appear to be suffering from strain and general tiredness."

In fact their condition was, as Balfour had pointed out, pretty symptomatic of all pilots in the combat area throughout Fighter Command. In the case of the RCAF pilots, however, there was another battle fatigue factor unique to this particular outfit — age. Most of them were well over the average age for a fighter pilot in the battle. Gordie McGregor at thirty-nine was the oldest Canadian in the fighting, and just possibly the oldest of any in Fighter Command to fly on operations in the Battle of Britain, period. Ernie McNab, thirty-four, and Hartland Molson, thirty-one, weren't far behind. Hardly spring chickens in a young man's game. (Not to exaggerate the point, but I finished my tour in 1944 after barely reaching my twenty-first birthday. Most of the time we did not stand on readiness and were given a generous share of leaves. Even at that, after a year-and-a-half on ops beginning when I was only nineteen, I was thoroughly exhausted.)

During the Battle of Britain, few pilots could be expected to last a third that long; in terms of flying hours, the fighter pilot's life expectancy was eighty-seven. On average, a pilot rarely got more than twenty-four hours off and only if he could be spared from steady availability, readiness and actual fighting. Any pilot kept in action for four months or more could be expected to be shot down (and probably killed or wounded) because (a) he was tired out, (b) he was stale, or (c) he had lost the will to fight. Hugh Dowding, a very sensitive individual, was acutely aware of all this and his did his best to juggle his squadrons around to allow some respite for his "chicks." But in September, and again in October, this wasn't easy. He also had an unwritten rule that no squadron leader should be older than twenty-six, though there is no evidence this was ever enforced.

Despite the fact that the overall issue had been decided on September 15, and September 27 had put a halt to massive daylight raids on London, there was no let-up in combat. For the moment, the Luftwaffe changed tactics to smaller bomber formations of thirty Junkers 88s escorted by 200 to 300 fighters. On September 28, the Germans launched two such attacks with London as the objective. That, in tackling one of these gaggles, the best the RAF could do was to only shoot down three German fighters was indicative of the how exhausted the pilots had become from the intensity of the demands made on them. Their losses of sixteen aircraft and nine pilots — among them John Boyle of Casselman, with 41 Squadron, whose record stood at four-and-a-fifth destroyed — to achieve such a paltry score was another manifestation of how serious their combat fatigue had become.

The Germans now switched to nuisance-type fighter sweeps, fighter-bomber attacks from high altitude. These were difficult to counter because, at over 25,000 feet, the new Messerschmitt 109 with a two-stage supercharger delivered a better performance than even the improved Hurricanes and Spitfires coming off the assembly lines. Moreover the raids, approaching from 20,000 feet or higher, minimized the effectiveness of British radar and were difficult for the Observer Corps to track, particularly on cloudy or hazy days. Commander Park's fighters had to struggle to altitude to engage the Germans, often long after they had crossed the coast. With the Germans always above them they were at the disadvantage of having to wait to be attacked. This necessitated standing patrols which compelled Park to keep his pilots in the air most of the time. It also meant wear and tear on machines and the crews who kept them flying.

But if the RAF was tired out so was the Luftwaffe, perhaps more so, and the era of German fighters over England was drawing to a close. The last major daylight air battle over Britain took place on the last day of September.

Between nine o'clock in the morning and five in the afternoon of September 30, the Luftwaffe launched five different raids made up of formations of bomb-carrying Messerschmitt 110s escorted by their single-engine 109 brothers, carrying 700- and 250-pound bombs respectively — scarcely an earth-shattering menace in terms of explosive power. Four of the raids were aimed at London and another on the Westland factory at Yeoville. It proved to be yet another day of hectic air fighting but this time it was a costly one for the Germans. Only thirty bombers got through to London all day. The attack on the Westland plant failed due to cloud cover. The Germans lost forty-seven aircraft. Casualties for the RAF totalled twenty fighters with eight pilots killed or wounded.

It was during the last combat of the day that the RCAF squadron added to its tally. At 4:20 p.m., Gordie McGregor led a wing patrol made up of three squadrons — his own, 303 and 229 — to cover Northolt at 20,000 feet. By 4:45, a swarm of Me 110s, escorted by 109s, appeared above the Hurricanes. Half the 109s swooped down to attack. McGregor held his course then turned to engage a Messerschmitt which had targeted one of his Hurricanes. As the Hurricane broke right, the 109 turned left, and McGregor opened fire. Towards the end of what he described as a "full burst," the enemy fighter streamed smoke and spun down into the clouds. Observers later confirmed that it crashed south of Brooklands.

In the same encounter, de Peyster Brown, who held the number two position in Green Section, saw several 109s approach from in front and, as they passed him, he was attacked by another from the rear. Cannon-shells shot away his left elevator and knocked a piece off his right wing-tip. The blast rocked the aircraft so badly that Brown temporarily lost control and it went into a spin. He fell 14,000 feet before he was able to pull out. Then, at 7,000 feet, he saw a 109 flying hell-bent-for-leather to the south. Brown slammed the throttle all the way forward and made a pass from the port stern-quarter where he let a barrage go from his Brownings. Chunks of fuselage fell off the German fighter and it seemed to stagger. Then it disappeared into a cloud layer. Brown followed the enemy plane into the overcast to try and find it but finally gave up. It was just as well he didn't linger. His own aircraft was so badly crippled he crashed on landing back at Northolt. However, he was given credit for damaging the 109.

That afternoon my father visited the squadron for the last time before flying back to Canada. On this occasion the RCAF maple leaf ensign was unfurled and flown for the first time outside Canadian soil. It was a short but moving ceremony for him — a result of his own contribution to its design as a staff officer in 1918 with the Canadian Air Force, the RCAF's predecessor. At the time he had suggested an insignia for the CAF consisting of a roundel with the maple leaf in the centre and promptly drew a sketch of it.

\*                  \*                  \*

On October 1, the Battle of Britain entered its final phase, and it was on this date that Johnny Kent fought his spectacular solo combat against forty German fighters. On the day following, Cowboy Blatchford made his first score since becoming the first Canadian to shoot down a German plane in WWII back in October 1939. Since that time, though he had not been in combat — he had been assigned to reconnaissance patrols — his life had not lacked for excitement. When the Germans invaded France, Blatchford found himself stranded at Orleans with the Germans only fifteen miles away. Somehow he managed to commandeer a Fairey Battle, a plane he had never flown before, and escape to England. But he was back in France next day at the controls of a Hudson transport to rescue some British army officers. During the early part of the Battle of Britain, while photographing an enemy aerodrome over Brittany at 6,000 feet, the engine of his Spitfire conked out. With flak frighteningly close all around him and unable to get his engine restarted, he decided to bail out. As he prepared himself for the leap, he realized he had lost over 5,000 feet of altitude and was down to 400 feet — too low to make a safe jump. The enemy flak had ceased and he could almost see the Germans gloating over the prospect of taking him prisoner as he landed wheels-up. Then, suddenly, his recalcitrant Rolls-Royce power-plant sprang to life and he was off and away at full throttle to flee the area, leaving showers of anti-aircraft bursts in his wake.

At the end of the summer, Blatchford was transferred to 41 Squadron flying Hurricanes from Debden. Only three days after joining the unit, he shared in the destruction of a Dornier 17, a German bomber rarely seen over England from then on.

The odds began to favour the Allies. Although there was no let-up in the bomber raids on October 2 — seventeen formations penetrated inland into the 11 Group area alone — the bombing results were neg- ligible. In fact, the Londoners regarded the daylight forays as nothing more than a nuisance and they no longer ran to the air-raid shelters when the sirens began to howl, but continued about their normal duties. The RAF had put up 154 patrols for a yield of seventeen enemy aircraft brought down at a loss of only one of its own. The strain was, in some degree, still there, but in spots there was some respite.

The Canadians with the Duxford Wing, for example, although they did fly regular patrols had not engaged a single enemy aircraft since September 27. At least they were spared the tension and dangers of combat, if not the rigour of hours of flying, staying alert, and waiting on readiness.

On October 3 and again on the 4th, the Luftwaffe began to reduce its efforts to fighter-bomber raids, singly or in pairs, although there was a steady stream throughout both days. On October 4 the RAF destroyed two Ju 88s in addition to ten Me 109s at a loss of only one aircraft.

Statistically this looked reassuring, but there still existed difficulties with the air defences as a bulletin issued that date from 11 Group commander, Keith Park, clearly illustrated. It also underlined the problems with wing formations. In part, it read:

> Tip-and-run raids across Kent by Me 110s carrying bombs and small formations of long-range bombers escorted by fighters give such short notice that the group controller is sometimes compelled to detail even single fighter squadrons before they attack aircraft factories, sector aerodromes, or other such vital points such as docks, Woolwich, etc. Normally however, group controller has sufficient time to detail from one to three pairs [two to six squadrons] to intercept raids heading for bombing targets in the vicinity of London.
>
> Whenever time permits I wish group controllers to get the readiness squadrons in company over the sector aerodromes, Spitfires 25,000 feet, Hurricanes 20,000 feet, and wait until they report they are in good position before sending them to patrol lines or to intercept raids having a good track in fairly clear weather.
>
> I wish the squadron commanders and sector controllers to know everything humanely possible is being done by groups to increase the warning of incoming raids. Meanwhile, squadrons can help by shortening the time of take-off, assembly and rendezvous with other squadrons to which they are detailed as pairs or wings.

That evening, No. 1 RCAF had occasion to hoist a few in honour of their CO, Ernie McNab, the second member of the RCAF to destroy an enemy aircraft and the first to lead a squadron in battle. He became the first in the service to win a war medal. During the afternoon word had come through that he had been awarded the DFC.

# CHAPTER TWENTY-ONE

# LAST CALL FOR THE CARIBOUS

October 5 drizzled miserably for most of the day, but that Saturday did have its bright moments both weatherwise and otherwise — particularly for the RCAF. By ten o'clock in the morning, two German raids of fifteen and twenty formations of fighters and bombers attacked West Malling and Detling airfields. But that was just a warm-up. The real action developed over Kent an hour and a half later when raids of twelve, thirty, forty and fifty enemy aircraft fanned out across south-eastern England to attack Detling again, as well as Folkestone on the coast.

Shortly after eleven o'clock, No. 1 Squadron RCAF and 303 Polish Squadron were vectored on a course southeast of Northolt by the sector controller to intercept the incursion. They climbed to 20,000 feet, and at 1:40 p.m., south of Maidstone and fifteen miles northwest of Folkestone, they sighted their quarry of what amounted to a thirty-plus assortment of Messerschmitt 109s and 110s.

Gordie McGregor, who was leading the wing formation, concentrated on an enemy section of seven 109s flying in loose line-astern. There were other bandits to the southeast, so he manipulated the two squadrons in between the seven German fighters and the coast and then attacked. At that instant the other German formation, made up of both Me 109s and 110s, joined in the fray and the sky immediately erupted into a series of vicious, whirring, twisting, turning, diving, climbing dogfights, one on one, spread over an altitude between 16,000 and 20,000 feet.

In the mêlée, McGregor was able to manoeuvre onto the tail of one of the single-engine fighters. His description of what happened next was terse and final. "After one burst of about eight seconds at very close range," he reported, "109 smoked and pilot bailed out." Chalk up another destroyed for the former Webster Trophy winner.

Paul Pitcher, who was leading the Search Section, had more luck than any of his squadron confrères that morning, though on his initial attack he failed to contact the enemy. He had lost height so he climbed to 21,000 feet to have a good look around. A wise tactic, height being one of the prime priorities of airfighting.

Near Canterbury he spotted four Me 109s in line-astern. Picking out the rear one, he closed in from the left until he was fully astern at 100 yards — then he let go. Firing three short bursts within twelve seconds he knocked pieces off the 109. Then its wheels dropped down and the aircraft rolled over onto its back. But Pitcher couldn't hang around to see the final result; three other 109s had jumped him from behind forcing him to break away. Suddenly, three Me 110s appeared in line-astern directly above him. From 280 yards he fired a four-second burst before he ran out of ammunition. Although he encountered heavy return fire from the rear-gunner, he saw his tracers strike the enemy aircraft which abruptly plunged towards the ground. Ground observers confirmed that the Me 109 Pitcher had first attacked had crashed west of Canterbury, but there was no sign of what happened to the Me 110. Pitcher was given a destroyed and a damaged.

Eric Beardmore, who along with Deane Nesbitt had rejoined the squadron four days earlier after recuperating in hospital from wounds sustained from being shot down and having to bail out in mid-September (both were on this patrol), flew as number three in Blue Section led by Dal Russel. As tail-end Charlie, he was the Me 109s' natural target. Tracer bullets whizzed by his ears. Beardmore broke sharply to port in a steep turn as Messerschmitts shot past him. He teamed up with another Hurricane from 303 Polish Squadron and they climbed to 18,000 feet where Beardmore saw an Me 110 at 5,000 feet below coming in from the southeast coast. Then, just as he was set to make his attack, he noticed five Me 109s headed southwest. Beardmore sighted on the rear one and opened fire; the rest of the German fighters started a slight turn to starboard. He drew within 150 yards of his target and fired again; this time, black smoke poured from the Messerschmitt's engine. It then pitched forward and dove to the ground. Beardmore didn't see it crash, and there was no confirmation. But he received credit for a damaged.

When the squadron became split up after the initial Me 109 attack, Green Section leader Bev Christmas decided to try his luck over the coast where he could see Messerschmitts and Hurricanes milling about. As he fixed his sights on an Me 110 coming north over the shore, four 109s shot across his nose at right angles. Christmas pulled around sharply behind them and fired at the leader. His aim was true. Smoke spewed from the Messerschmitt and pieces of the fuselage fell off as the fighter started into a shallow dive. Christmas let go another spurt of fire, this time aimed at the cockpit. It probably killed the pilot; the aircraft went into a vertical dive still trailing smoke, and crashed into a field near Hawkinge.

It had been a rewarding outing for the Caribous. Count: three destroyed, three damaged, their third most successful day. But the downside was one pilot wounded. Hartland Molson had been hit in the leg and was forced to take to his chute, alighting near Charthouse where he was taken to Canterbury Hospital to recover.*

Another Canadian who also put up a commendable show that day was a sergeant-pilot flying Spitfires with 66 Squadron at Gravesend. Rufus Ward, the only Canadian non-commissioned officer to fight in the Battle of Britain, was credited with probably destroying an Me 109 and damaging two others. His glory was fleeting. Next day he was killed in action.

That day, the weather was typical of late fall in England, dull with continuous rain which, apart from the skirmishes already noted, kept Luftwaffe activity in general to a minimum. However, it did not prevent a Junkers 88 raider from popping out of the clouds at 300 feet around 3:35 p.m. to drop a 1,000-pound bomb on Northolt aerodrome. No. 1 Squadron RCAF's diarist's report of the incident, in his own inimitable fashion, gave a graphic picture of some of the conditions under which the fighter squadrons laboured.

> The 1,000 pounder did some damage to both hangars, smashed two Hurricanes and killed a sergeant-pilot of 303 Squadron and one of the station defence airmen. The station defence was unable to get a crack at the marauder as no one told them that the raider was coming, or their guns were not loaded, or the corporal wasn't there to give the order to fire, or something. Words stronger than a "poor show" are required here to describe our reception to this marauder and here they are — it was a goddamn awful bloody balls-up.

*          *          *

*By a strange quirk of fate I happened to be in Ottawa on leave from my last year at boarding school before joining the RCAF when my father was informed (on the Sunday) of Molson's misfortune. I remember clearly to this day him telephoning Molson's wife in Montreal immediately he had the details, and the words he used. "He's in the hospital and he's safe. He's fine, he's going to be all right. There's nothing to worry about." This related incident brought the Battle of Britain home to an impressionable youth who was avidly following it day by day.

On October 7, Pete Lochnan ran up the squadron's final victory in the Battle of Britain which brought his personal tally to one-and-two thirds destroyed, and four damaged. Visibility was good and the Luftwaffe was busy with a smattering of raids ranging from the main targets of London and Merseyside in the south and from Harwich and Newcastle to the Firth of Forth in the north. No. 1 Squadron RCAF was assigned the job of patrolling over Biggin Hill at 1:30 p.m., that airfield being the target.

The Hurricanes were at 20,000 feet over Rochester when they sighted about ten Me 109s heading west in the opposite direction to the Caribous. Lochnan broke formation, wheeled about and gave chase. Seeing him bearing down on them, the German pilots split up going off in all directions. Lochnan tagged on to one of them steering south.

From the port side, directly behind the enemy fighter, Lochnan fired a long burst raking the aircraft with his bullets. As pieces flew off the wings and fuselage, he opened up from the opposite quarter. This time his bullets set the aircraft on fire and it went down aflame in a shallow dive. But in the process Lochnan had been attacked twice by Me 109s and had to lunge into a spiral dive to shake them off his tail. As he pulled out, his engine started to rattle and, because he was also out of ammunition, he landed at Biggin Hill. However after making a minor adjustment to his Merlin motor, and rearming, he flew back to base.

On the other hand Deane Nesbitt, who had sustained multiple hits to his Hurricane and had also landed at Biggin Hill, had to leave his aircraft there for repairs.

This was the last patrol for No. 1 RCAF in the Battle of Britain. The next day, October 8, orders were received to proceed to Prestwick in Scotland after a relief squadron arrived. They came none too soon as No. 1 pilots had pretty well reached the end of their tethers. Suffering from nervous exhaustion, they were completely worn out. Later, looking back, Hartland Molson described the squadron as a "well-knit unit with some pride in ourselves, some sadness and concern at our casualties, and a growing conviction that the battle was going our way." He also added, "I think we were constantly surprised that we were able to hold together. In retrospect, I feel that we represented the country not too badly."

To put it mildly. The Caribous' record during the fifty-three days between August 17 and October 9, 1940, was indeed commendable considering the average age of the pilots and their lack of training. Starting with its first kill on August 26, the squadron destroyed thirty German planes, probably destroyed eight, and damaged thirty-five. Three pilots

— Bob Edwards, Ross Smither and Otto Peterson — were killed, and three others were wounded. On average, when weather permitted, the unit flew three to four patrols a day. It is a credit, too, to the ground crew. Working under strained conditions, they kept those Hurricanes flying throughout the tour of operations. As an appropriate wrap-up to the squadron's part in the battle, the night before No. 1 RCAF flew north, news arrived that both Gordie McGregor and Dal Russel had been awarded the DFC.

# CHAPTER TWENTY-TWO

# ROUND-UP TIME

By the time the Caribous packed it in and headed north from the combat zone, whether they realized or not — or for that matter cared — the Luftwaffe had been thoroughly defeated, a fact that even Hermann Goering was forced to accept. But how could the failure in the air be explained to the troops? to the German people? It called for all the propaganda skills that Dr. Joseph Goebbels, that master of cover-up and mind manipulation, could summon and bring to bear.

The solution was simple. The Big Lie, of course. The Battle of Britain never happened. There was no such thing. Goering publicly dismissed air operations against the British Isles as "merely the initial phase" and went on to outline the plan for "absolute control of the Channel and the English coastal areas." At the same time he demanded "progressive and complete annihilation of London with all its military objectives and industrial production."

On October 12, Wilhelm Keitel, chief of the Combined German General Staff, issued an official bulletin making known Hitler's decision to postpone the invasion:

> The Fuehrer has decided that from now on until the spring, preparations for Sea Lion shall be continued solely for the purpose of maintaining political and military pressure on England.
>
> Should the invasion be reconsidered in the spring or early summer of 1941, orders for a renewal of operational readiness will be issued later.

While the transfer of the Caribous to Scotland created an RCAF absence from the scene, during the closing twenty-three days of the Battle of Britain there were still plenty of pilots left with the RAF to carry the Canadian banner in the air-fighting, not without the inevitable casualties.

One of these occurred on the day the Caribous received their transfer orders. George Corbett with 66 Squadron, who had a score of one aircraft destroyed and another probably destroyed, became a fatality.

On the brighter side, on October 9, the day after the Canadian squadron left Northolt, Jim Walker of Gletchen, Alta., flying a Spitfire with 41 Squadron from Hornchurch, brought down a Messerschmitt 109 to add to the one he had destroyed with another pilot two days earlier.

Three days later, on the date Hitler publicly called off plans for the invasion, despite mist and fog the Germans flew 797 sorties between 6:45 a.m. and the late afternoon. In a day of almost uninterrupted air activity, the Luftwaffe lost eleven planes to the RAF's ten. One of the RAF's victories went to Canada. John Hart, a native of Sackville, N.B., shared in the destruction of a Junkers 88 bomber with two of his 602 Squadron mates.

The Canadian star of the show at this late stage in the game, however, proved to be the Montrealer who had won the DFC as a bomber pilot. Bill Nelson had already posted a score of two aircraft destroyed and two damaged during the month of August. Now, on three different occasions over the next two weeks, he would destroy three more enemy planes — all of them Me 109s — to make him an Ace. The first of these was on October 17, a day of limited visibility that saw both large and small concentrations of enemy fighters and fighter-bombers penetrating inland throughout the day. It was during one of those incursions that Nelson shot down a 109.

But it was day of tragedy, also. That Thursday, Canada lost two of her sons in combat.

Up until this time, 242 Squadron had seen no action since September 27, when Canadians with the unit accounted for two German planes destroyed, one probably shot down, and one damaged. Now, four weeks later, Red Section, made up of Neil Campbell, Marvin Brown and a British pilot who led it, was scrambled from Coltishall at 8:45 a.m. to patrol off Yarmouth. As soon as they got airborne they were ordered to land. Bad omen. A false alarm; the instruction was quickly rescinded. At 9:07 the section was given a vector to head southeast and told to climb to 7,000 feet. Eight minutes later the pilots spotted a Dornier 17 bomber 3,000 feet below them, flying south.

With the English pilot in the vanguard, the three Hurricanes swooped down to attack. The leader delivered a quick burst then broke away. Brown's turn came next and from dead-astern he fired, too. But at that precise moment well-aimed bullets from the German rear-gunner's 7.9mm machine-guns struck Brown's throttle controls, jamming the quadrant forward, wide open. He had no choice but to break off and head home. It left Campbell all alone to grapple with the enemy bomber, a tussle from which he never returned. But neither the British pilot who lost the Dornier in the clouds, or Brown, who had landed back at Coltishall, were on hand to witness what happened. Later Campbell's body and his Hurricane were hauled out of the water thirty miles off Yarmouth. He had obviously been the target of the same accurate fire the enemy rear-gunner had inflicted on Brown's aircraft, and had crashed into the sea.

The other Canadian casualty that day was Hugh Reilly whose home was London, Ont. He was killed while flying a Spitfire with 66 Squadron from Gravesend. Campbell's and Reilly's demise represented the last Canadian fatalities in the Battle of Britain. It brought total Canadian casualties to twenty.

A week later Hilly Brown shared in the destruction of a Do 17 with another pilot from No. 1 Squadron RAF. Three days afterwards, the relentless Bill Nelson brought down an Me 109. Then, on October 29, he destroyed another, his third in twelve days. On the same date, Butch Barton proved himself just as resolute when he shot down one Me 109 and damaged another. It brought his final total in the battle two three-and-a-half aircraft destroyed, two-and-a-half probably destroyed, and a whopping eight damaged.

October 30 saw enemy activity sharply reduced. At noon, two waves of fifty and sixty raiders flew up the Thames estuary and, late in the afternoon, a series of raids amounting to 130 aircraft crossed the coast, a few of which reached London. Dick Lewis, a Hurricane pilot from Vancouver with No. 1 Squadron RAF, wrote the swan song to Canada's part in the Battle of Britain when he won his only victory by shooting down a Ju 88 bomber.

In the 114 days the Battle of Britain lasted — July 10 to October 31 — 100 Canadian pilots served with one RCAF squadron and forty-six RAF squadrons. In round figures they had accounted for 130 German airplanes destroyed, thirty probably destroyed, and more than seventy damaged. Canada had made the second-largest contribution of any Commonwealth country and the third-largest of all the Allied nations.

On October 31, sporadic rainshowers fell as if to douse the dying embers of a conflagration that a small but brave and determined band of Allied pilots, at heavy sacrifice, had fought so desperately to put out. By sunset the cinders had died to ashes. In history's logbook that was it. The Battle of Britain had drawn to a close. It was all over except for the shouting.

# CHAPTER TWENTY-THREE

# OUTGROWTH

On March 15, 1941, Gordie McGregor led 402 Squadron RCAF on the first Canadian fighter sweep over enemy occupied territory covering the Boulogne sector of the Pas de Calais in northern France. The switch to the offensive had been abrupt with repercussions at the highest level of Fighter Command. With the Battle of Britain won, an impatient Winston Churchill wanted swift fighter retaliation and revenge against the Germans. This brought about a major shift in the RAF hierarchy.

The Big Wing controversy erupted in a frenzy. There were recriminations all round. Off with their heads! Even Douglas Bader, a mere squadron leader, was brought into the act. But it all occurred within respected military discipline procedures. It was a carefully rehearsed and and staged scenario, a convenient *cause célèbre* that had been in the cards for sometime. Hugh Dowding, as head of Fighter Command, and Keith Park, commander of 11 Group, were defence specialists. Now that their services were no longer required, they were summarily removed without fanfare and replaced by the more combative Sholto Douglas and Trafford Leigh-Mallory.

This changing of the guard directly affected the growth of RCAF fighter strength, for which the groundwork had been laid in the Battle of Britain, and its eventual extension into reconnaissance and tactical bombing. Its emergence began with the formation of the Canadian Digby Wing on April 14, 1941, made up of 401 Squadron (née No. 1) commanded by Deane Nesbitt and 402 Squadron (formerly No. 2) under the command of Vaughan Corbett. Both units had been renumbered on March 1, making them two of the first three members of the RCAF overseas "400-block" squadrons. The other entry was 400 (Army Cooperation) Squadron, formerly No. 100, which had arrived in England in February 1940. Gordie McGregor took over the Digby Wing, making him the first with the RCAF title of Wing Commander Flying.

Later in the year Cowboy Blatchford, the first Canadian fighter pilot to open fire on an enemy plane in WWII, took over from McGregor to became the first Canadian in the RAF to command an RCAF fighter wing. Earlier, Blatchford had flown on the first Rhubarb, a two-man low-level attack against enemy coastal ground targets. These pinprick raids were Churchill's idea of keeping the Germans on the defensive. To some degree they may have accomplished that objective, but for the most part they proved fruitless and horrendously costly, some of the best fighter pilots being lost in executing them.

As an example, on January 12, Willie McKnight and his wingman were strafing German troops near Gravelines when they were bounced by Me 109s. One latched onto McKnight's tail. His wingman managed to get in a quick squirt at the enemy plane before both disappeared into a cloud. But McKnight was never seen again. Thus the life of a pilot with eighteen victories to his credit and the top Canadian ace in the Battle of Britain was thoughtlessly and uselessly wasted. It was not until the fall of 1943 that, over the vigorous objections of the obstinate Leigh-Mallory, these senseless forays were finally curtailed.*

During 1941, five new fighter squadrons and one new army cooperation squadron were established, the forerunners of thirty-five RCAF squadrons to be formed overseas. Two of the fighter units were attached to the Digby Wing. Three veteran Battle of Britain pilots were assigned as COs: Paul Pitcher initially headed up 411 Squadron and then was shortly relieved by Stan Turner, the first Canadian RAF pilot to command an RCAF fighter squadron; and Charles Trevena, an ex-"Caribou," took over 412 Squadron.

In March of the following year, Pitcher took command of 417 Squadron which was transferred to Egypt where he became the first to lead an RCAF unit in the desert. Later, during the Sicilian and Italian campaigns, Stan Turner again followed in Pitcher's slipstream, to serve as the squadron's CO for the last six months of 1943.

In April 1942, another RCAF fighter squadron was formed — the eighth and last to be established in the U.K. — and at the end of the same year the Canadian Kenley Wing came into being. During that time Ernie McNab, the RCAF's first ace and first to be decorated for combat, became Station Commander at Digby. By this time, Canadians in both the RCAF and RAF had become firmly entrenched in England ready

---

*It took no less a fighter authority than Johnnie Johnson, the leading Allied Ace in WWII in the European Theatre, to convince Fighter Command of their futility.

for the major reorganization that took place in 1943 in preparation for the invasion of Europe.

In June, with the formation of the RAF Second Tactical Air Force, two Canadian Airfields — later redesignated (Fighter) Wings — were established, each comprising three RCAF Spitfire squadrons. Dal Russel, who in the Battle of Britain had been one of the first of three RCAF pilots to be awarded the DFC, took over as Wing Commander (Wingco) Flying of 126 Airfield, made up of his old Squadron 401 along with 411 and 412.

In February 1941, Russel had been repatriated to Canada where he joined 118 Squadron stationed at Rockliffe in Ottawa. Later, when it moved to Dartmouth, N.S, he gained new prominence by flying a Hurricane bedecked with tail struts as well as Black Crosses and Swastikas painted on the wings and fuselage to resemble a Messerschmitt 109 for shooting an episode in Warner Brothers' movie *Captains of the Clouds*, a story about Canadian bush pilots who joined the RCAF. In the final scene, the Me 109 shoots down a bomber (a twin-engine Anson trainer "flown" by Dennis Morgan and Jimmy Cagney) being ferried to England off the Irish coast. Filmed not far out to sea from the shores of Nova Scotia, Russel had the ultimate irony of playing the part of the pilot of an aircraft masquerading as a type he had fought against a year earlier, one of which he had succeeded in destroying on September 27, 1940. Having completed the last film take, Russel proceeded to buzz the main street of Halifax at low level going full out, scaring the hell out of folks who, seeing the German markings, mistook the Hurricane for the real thing.

Simultaneously with the establishment of the first two RCAF Fighter Airfields, Second TAF also incorporated into its fold two others, one to be later designated a (Reconnaissance) Wing to which 400 Squadron, the first RCAF unit to arrive in Britain in WWII, was attached. The other, to be renamed (a Fighter-Bomber) Wing), was made up of two other former Army Cooperation squadrons, one of which had been formed in January.

Subsequently in the winter of 1943-44, Second TAF established two new RCAF Airfields — Fighter and Fighter-Bomber Wings — each comprising three squadrons formed in Canada with a nucleus of combat-hardened pilots, sent directly overseas complete with ground crews. Deane Nesbitt, former CO of 401 Squadron, took administrative command of the 144 Fighter Wing in May after the original airfield commander was killed.

By D-Day the six RCAF fighter, fighter-bomber and fighter-reconnaissance wings had fifteen squadrons on the battle-line to make up the 83 Group of the Second TAF in support of the Second British Army while 84 Group, which contained no Canadian squadrons, supported the First Canadian Army.

On the surface that would appear fatuous. However, solid reasoning lay behind that decision which was most flattering to say the least. Before the war, RAF strategy was based on the tunnel-vision concept of massive bombing attacks against their enemy's homeland with fighters ready to defend should the need arise. The swift *Blitzkrieg* successes by the Luftwaffe brought about a reappraisal of the air force's role when it became very apparent how effectively it could be employed as a ground-support arm. It was first used successfully in this manner by the RAF in Egypt in support of the British Eighth Army. This experience resulted in the creation of the Second Tactical Air Force with most of the squadrons drawn from Fighter Command and the formation of new squadrons.

Originally it had been intended that an all-Canadian composite group would support the First Canadian Army. But because of the demanding role assigned the British Second Army in assaulting the beaches of Normandy, on January 26, 1944 the decision was taken that it would need the support of the strongest, most experienced tactical air group and that meant the one made up of RCAF squadrons. The toughest and the best for the job. Thus, a dream of Canadian ground and air forces working together never came to fruition.

By the beginning of July, with twelve fighter squadrons stationed on air strips in Normandy, two veteran Battle of Britain pilots were given senior commands. In October 1943, Dal Russel had been taken off ops as 126 Airfield's Wingco Flying and given a desk job. Not for long. Dropping his rank by half a stripe, by April 1944 he had wheedled his way back into the fray as the CO of one of the squadrons sent out from Canada — No. 442. Not for long there, either. In July, in Normandy, he got his old job back as Wingco Flying of what by then had been redesignated 126 (Fighter) Wing. At the same time, Gordie McGregor, the RCAF's first Wingco Flying, became the wing's Airfield Commander.

At the turn of the year, Stan Turner, who up to that time had commanded an RAF wing in Italy, became Airfield Commander of 127 Fighter Wing, while Deane Nesbitt took over command of 143 Fighter Bomber Wing.

In Europe, between the end of the Battle of Britain and the end of the war, four of its Canadian veterans, three of them RCAF and one RAF, were made Station/Airfield Commanders: McNab, McGregor, Nesbitt (twice) and Turner (RAF). Two RCAF pilots reached Wingco Flying status — McGregor (the first Canadian) and Russel (twice) — while three Canadians in the RAF served in the same capacity: Cowboy Blatchford (RCAF wing), Hilly Brown and Stan Turner. Both Blatchford and Brown were killed in action; all the rest survived.

Dal Russel and Stan Turner fought in WWII from start to finish, Russel amassing an amazing 286 operational sorties, Turner with an incredible 1,125 hours and 35 minutes combat time. On one occasion Turner was wounded, but Russel never so much as suffered a scratch. A rare species of lunge and luck laced with a generous portion of guts.

Skeets Ogilvie, the "Palace Guardian" who downed the Dornier that bombed Buckingham Palace on Battle of Britain Day, enjoyed his own brand of lunge and luck. He not only got out of a German POW camp during the Great Escape, but he lived to tell about it. With a score of three enemy aircraft destroyed, three probables, and two damaged to his credit, the Spitfire pilot was shot down over France on July 11, 1941. Badly wounded, he was hospitalized for nine months before being taken to Stalag Luft III where he became one of the prisoners engaged in tunnelling. On the night of March 24, 1944, Ogilvie was the last of seventy-six to crawl out of the tunnel before a German sentry stumbled into the exit. Roaming the countryside for two days he was recaptured and sent to another prison camp. He was lucky. Fifty of the others were brutally murdered by the Gestapo after being taken back into custody.

*          *          *

After the war, many of the Splendid Hundred continued to distinguish themselves both in military life and on civvy street. Johnny Kent, who single-handedly had taken on forty Messerschmitts, remained with the RAF after the war and was appointed personal staff officer to the Military Governor of British Occupied Germany. In 1956 he retired from the service but stayed in Britain to take up a position in the aviation electronics industry.

Ernie McNab, who was the second RCAF pilot to go into action, was also the last of the Battle of Britain pilots to leave the Canadian air force, when he retired in 1957 after nearly thirty years of service.

Gordie McGregor, the former Webster trophy winner, became the first full-time president of Trans-Canada Air Lines (later Air Canada), a post he held for twenty years. He also served as president of the International Aviation Transport Association and as a member of the advisory board of the RCAF Association.

Hartland Molson, one of the first Canadians in the Battle of Britain to take to his parachute when he was forced to bail out after an altercation with a Messerschmitt 110, ended the war as director of personnel at RCAF

Headquarters in Ottawa. Following the close of hostilities he returned to the family brewery business, and in July 1955 was called to the Canadian Senate where he held a seat until retiring from the house in 1993.

Deane Nesbitt, twice shot down in the Battle of Britain, rejoined the family firm of Nesbitt, Thomson and Co., and held the presidency for twenty-five years. During that time he handled the financing of Trans-Canada Pipelines.

Peter O'Brian, the only Canadian ever to be awarded the Cranwell RAF College's coveted Sword of Honour, rose to become RAF Fighter Command Group Captain of Operations. In 1958 he became aide-de-camp to the Queen in London before retiring to Toronto the following year.

Stan Turner transferred to the RCAF following the war holding a number of posts including that of Canadian Air Attaché to Moscow. On retiring from the service he became an executive with the planning staff of EXPO 67 in Montreal, Quebec.

\*          \*          \*

## POST MORTEM

In 1977, the Sussex and Surrey Aviation Historical Society recovered the wreckage of a German Junkers 88 twin-engine bomber. On investigation, the place and type of aircraft was found to match up with the 88 Gordie McGregor had claimed as a probable on September 27, 1940 (see page 93). This brought his total of enemy aircraft destroyed to five, making the oldest pilot to fight in the Battle of Britain an ace at last, thirty-seven years after his victory. A belated salute!

# CHAPTER TWENTY—FOUR

# THE RECORD

The record of Canadian courage in the Battle of Britain is, in a sense, isolated — just as the battle itself, in the context of the Second World War, is an insular instance also. So to properly appreciate the full significance of what the Battle of Britain meant, and the role the Canadians played, it must be viewed from a detached perspective. It is therefore necessary to retrace the flight path back to the time of Dunkirk.

After the British had successfully evacuated their army, Hitler, all powerful now that he dominated the Continent, was certain that with the threat of an invasion, Britain would sue for peace leaving the Wehrmacht free to attack Russia. Goering assured him that the Luftwaffe could knock out the RAF in four days. Flushed with its successes as a terror weapon — Guernica in Spain, the first city to be obliterated by aerial bombing, Warsaw, then Rotterdam, as well as air artillery support for the Blitzkriegs on Poland, Norway, Belgium, Holland and France — its leaders had become so confident that they let their accomplishments colour their judgment. They so seriously overrated the capacity of their air arm that they looked across the English Channel as if it was just one more river to cross, like the Meuse. In reality they faced a major air battle, something for which the Luftwaffe had neither been designed nor equipped for, and consequently was lamentably unprepared.

Furthermore, the invasion fleet was scarcely more than a myth, a ragtag collection of boats, barges and rafts without proper troop and tank landing craft that characterized the later Allied assault flotillas. But had it not been for Dowding's astute generalship, and Goering, Kesselring and Sperrle's lack of it (along with their failure to recognize the importance of radar or to understand modern aerial tactics), the Germans might, just might, have succeeded in winning the Battle of Britain.

If Commander Park had not husbanded his fighters so frugally, and if Goering had concentrated on destroying the British radar chain as well as the sector control stations, with its communications system out of business the RAF couldn't have lasted very long. That accomplished, the Luftwaffe could have blown the Home Fleet out of the water. And, just as they had done in Norway and the Netherlands, the Germans could have landed parachutists to pave the way for an invasion force. Once ashore, in the face of a virtually unarmed Imperial Army, the Wehrmacht could have walked to Westminster.

What prevented it is that the Germans had no game plan for a drawn-out air battle. Kesselring and Sperrle, the Luftflotte commanders, simply took events one day at a time and had no comprehensive strategic plan. Goering had deluded himself that, with the Luftwaffe's Messerschmitt 109 fighter, he could easily sweep the RAF's Hurricanes and Spitfire aside. It is true that the Me 109 was marginally the best fighter in the Battle of Britain and accounted for most of the losses sustained by Fighter Command. It was as fast as the Spitfire, considerably faster than the Hurricane, and could out-climb and out-dive both of them as well as enjoy a higher-altitude capability. Equipped with cannon, it was far more formidable than the British fighters.

On the other hand, Allied fighter pilots had little to fear from the German bombers which were poorly armed and could rarely bring more than one gun to bear on an attacking fighter. (All this is discussed in detail in the following section, "Apparatus Belli.") But the point here is that Goering seriously underestimated the spirit of the Allied pilots and the determination of their ground crews to keep their planes flying, and he never bothered to study or appraise the brilliant tactics employed by their commanders.

In the final analysis, the RAF did not defeat the Luftwaffe in the Battle of Britain. What it did accomplish was to inflict such unacceptable losses that it denied the Germans their objective of invading England. They had been stopped in their tracks for the first time. For their part, the Nazi Germans typically and Teutonically denied that any such epic battle ever took place. They brushed off the entire exercise as merely a series of raids which had proven so unsuccessful that they had simply turned their attention elsewhere. In truth, they got thrashed so badly the Battle of Britain saw the end of the Luftwaffe's reputation as an invincible force.

In any event, Hitler had little interest in the battle after his fighters and bombers were defeated. What really concerned him most was that his coastal defences from the tip of Norway to the Spanish border were intact so that his U-boats could be allowed to starve and strangle Britain far more effectively than any air war could do. That established, he turned his back on his western phalanx and aimed his sights eastward — and began pouring over maps of Russia.

The most significant, far-reaching result of the Battle of Britain is that it converted American opinion to a belief that the British, given help, might win. In military terms it proved that Great Britain was a secure base from which the United States could fight Germany and that air power was the decisive weapon with which to wage the fight.

The heroism displayed by the Splendid Hundred in helping to bring this about, out of all proportion to their numbers, is one that must never be forgotten. They were the cream of Canada's crop. *Per Ardua Ad Astra* (Through Adversity to the Stars).

# DEBRIEFING

## I / *Apparatus Belli*

To paraphrase: Never in the field of military aeronautical development was so much accomplished in so short a time by so few. In Europe, between 1931 and 1936, a handful of brilliant aircraft builders and designers — Sydney Camm, Claudius Dornier, Ernst Heinkel, Hugo Junkers, Willy Messerschmitt, Reginald Mitchell, and among them a Canadian engineer from Toronto, Beverley Shenston — magically transformed the concept of the rickety wood-and-wire, canvas-and-glue machines of the First World War into the sleek metal monoplane fighters and bombers that would decide the Battle of Britain in the Second.

It was a difference of light years. Speeds of more than 300 miles an hour. Ceilings up to 40,000 feet. Bomb loads 5,000 pounds and higher. Multi-armament, including cannon. As many as eight synchronized rapid-firing machine-guns installed in the wings of a fighter. Bombers with cannon mounted on top of the fuselage or under it. Enclosed cockpits. Armour plating for protection and bulletproof windscreens. Retractable undercarriages. Variable-pitch propellers that meant greater control on take-off and landing, and maximum battle speed. Precision instruments with automatic gyro horizons to allow blind flying in the worst weather conditions. Air-to-air and air-to-ground radio contact. And rapid developments and refinements during the war: radar detection and range finding in flight. A remarkable metamorphosis!

Displayed together, the aircraft flown during the Battle of Britain were a diverse lot, each with its own hallmark.

Among the single-engine fighters, the Hurricane stands out as the sturdiest of all three. To begin with, it is larger and several feet taller than the others. Its wide-track undercarriage, thick lateral wings, and a slight hunch to the spine add to its formidable appearance.

By contrast, the Messerschmitt 109 and the Spitfire are smaller. Both are narrower in wingspan by four to six feet than the Hurricane, and shorter in length by six to eleven. But there the similarity ends. In appearance, they could not be more unalike. The first impression you get of the Me 109 is that it looks like a flying engine. Its huge Daimler Benz engine dominates its angular structure, giving it a ferocious look. Its stubby wings, squared off at the tips, its wheels and struts awkwardly splayed outwards, and the square, metal-framed cockpit hood are all business but hardly make it a thing of beauty.

*Gloster Gladiator II*

By comparison, the Spitfire, with its graceful wings in a classic elliptical configuration, and its smooth, rounded, flush-riveted metal skin, gives it a look of refinement. Its wheels close together and thin, short struts, add to its deceptive air of fragility.

The Defiant, also a single-engine fighter although it packs a crew of two — an air-gunner as well as a pilot — in most respects resembles the Hurricane which it deliberately copied. In size and in length, they are almost exact, and its wings are similar in shape. Silhouetted from the side, the fore and aft sections are almost identical, but the profile is jarred by a gun-turret directly behind the cockpit. Another difference is the spats added to the wheel section.

In the twin-engine fighter category, the British and German designs have little or nothing in common, although the Blenheim and Messerschmitt 110 are almost the same size. The Blenheim has tapered wings and rounded wingtips, an upper-gun turret amidships, a large, arch-shaped tail, and is powered by two large radial engines. The machine looks heavy and lumbering.

The Me 110, on the other hand, is sleek and speedy looking, with two in-line engines. Its wings are straight, the wingtips are squared, and it has a tail section with twin rudders. But its most striking feature is the large, glassed-in housing for the cockpit and the air-gunner.

Among the twin-engine bombers, the Heinkel 111, with its enormous glass nose, is the most domineering of all three. A wingspan of seventy-five feet and an overall length of sixty feet makes it by far the largest as well. For a medium bomber, it is quite awesome and solid-looking with clean, semi-symmetrical lines and elliptically shaped wings.

The Dornier 17 (and 215) is aptly named — the "Flying Pencil." Its long, thin, rounded fuselage, twin rudders and high monoplane wing give it the look of a racer. Even its large radial engines and a nose bristling with guns fail to detract from its classic elegance.

The Junkers 88 is, in a word, rugged. Hostile as can be. The same size as the Dornier, there is nothing gentle about it. It has a large nose section, strong thick wings, a substantial tail section, and two powerful in-line engines housed in radial cowlings.

Viewed from almost any angle, the single-engine Junkers 87 can only be described as an ugly duckling. Cranked wings with spats covering the wheels, it also has a clumsy looking tail. Large glass canopies cover the two adjoining cockpits of the pilot and gunner. It is a graceless-looking machine.

Appearances are only skin-deep, however; behind each aircraft's design lie technological advances meant to make it a superior fighting weapon. The Battle of Britain was their first real testing ground.


## BRISTOL BLENHEIM

One can only speculate what Andrew Fletcher of Lethbridge, Alta. might have accomplished at the controls of a bona fide fighter. As it turned out, during the Battle of Britain, as the pilot of one of the unwieldy twin-engine Blenheims, he succeeded in destroying two enemy fighters — a Messerschmitt 109 and a 110 — as well as damaging a Heinkel 115 seaplane. An astounding feat given the inept equipment he was saddled with, one for which he richly deserved the DFC awarded him.

Indirectly, as a fighter, the Blenheim owed its origin to Lord Rothermere who, in 1934, ordered a prototype of a new civil aviation transport capable of seating eight passengers from the Bristol Aeroplane Company. On delivery it was discovered that it could attain the then-astonishing speed of 307 miles an hour. Rothermere made a gift of the aircraft, known as the "Britain First," to the nation. Better he should have kept it. With modifications it first went into production as a light bomber, renamed the Blenheim. But these changes and additions greatly increased the weight and shaved nearly fifty miles an hour off its top speed. However, its sturdiness and airworthiness prompted the boffins at the Air Ministry in its wisdom to order a number as fighters, a role for which it was lamentably unsuited. Powered by two 840-hp Bristol Mercury nine-cylinder air-cooled engines, it had a wingspan of fifty-six feet, four inches and was nearly forty feet long. It had an armoured nose and four 303-calibre Browning machine-guns mounted under the fuselage to fire forward, and a single one mounted in the port wing as well as a Vickers gun firing aft from a dorsal turret. Its maximum speed of between 260 and 284 miles an hour was no match for the Me 109 or even the 110. It should have stayed a fleet passenger plane because it certainly was no fighter and never had much manoeuvrability in the first place.

During the Battle of Britain, the seven Blenheim-equipped RAF fighter squadrons, four Canadian pilots among them, could contribute very little to the fighting, the rare exception being Andrew Fletcher, and their casualties proved that the British Air Ministry's theory that it was better to put anything into the air than nothing was no more than a costly fallacy.

The Blenheim was later transferred to a night-fighter role. But here it failed as well because its speed was not sufficient to catch the German bombers onto which it was vectored.

*Bristol Blenheim*

# BOULTON PAUL DEFIANT

The Defiant never should have happened. Born on the principle of surprise, a premise that is at best fleeting, it was the product of a misguided concept to begin with. Of three Canadians, all with 141 Squadron, who had the misfortune to pilot this ill-conceived excuse for a fighter, only two survived and they were just plain lucky to get away with it.

The idea was to duplicate the Hurricane as closely as possible so that at first glance it would be mistaken for it. Then, when an enemy fighter attacked from above and astern he would be "surprised" by four hydraulically operated machine-guns blasting away at him from a turret to the rear of the cockpit. That was the Defiant's only armament, however. There were no forward-firing guns. In front, it was as helpless as it was useless.

Built by Boulton Paul Aircraft Limited to Air Ministry specifications, the Defiant had the same powerplant as its clone, a 1,030-hp Rolls-Royce Merlin engine, and was about the same size overall.

On May 29, 1940, during the Dunkirk evacuation, the ruse worked perfectly. Wedged in among the Hurricanes, two squadrons of Defiants destroyed thirty-seven German planes. But the success was shortlived. The Germans weren't deceived for long. They soon discovered that they could attack unimpeded head-on or underneath from the rear. This was coupled with the fact that the weight of an extra passenger in the form of an air-gunner and the Defiant's lack of manoeuvrability rendered it completely vulnerable and unprotected. From then on, the Defiants were dead ducks. The final blow fell on July 19, the first — and last — time the Defiant was used in the Battle of Britain.

That afternoon while patrolling over Folkestone, 141 Squadron was bounced by a *Jagdstaffel* of Messerschmitt 109s. Within a matter of seconds the unit was virtually decimated. Six planes were shot down and four pilots and six gunners killed — among them Alex Howley of Victoria. Had it not been for the intervention of Hurricanes that came to their rescue, Duke Arthur of Winnipeg and Arthur Smith of Summerland, B.C., would have shared a similar fate.

But 141 as a unit was completely shattered. Several days later it was posted north where the Defiants were assigned the role of night-fighters. They proved almost equally inadequate in this capacity as well and eventually ended up towing drogue targets for air-firing practice.

*Boulton Paul Defiant*

## DORNIER 17

Ostensibly designed as a high-speed passenger and mail carrier for Luf-thansa Airlines, when the Dornier 17 first took to the air as a bomber in 1935, aerodynamically it was the most advanced airplane in the world. During the Spanish Civil War, it made a good account of itself even though it quickly became apparent that, when unescorted by fighters, it was highly vulnerable to the Republican forces' Russian-built *Polikarpov* fighters. In the Battle of Britain, however, it failed to live up to expectations due to lack of armament and inferior speed to the RAF fighters. As an example, Canadians, nine of them flying Hurricanes, three piloting Spitfires, shot down six Do 17s, probably destroyed one, damaged two more, and shared in putting six others out of action, without suffering a single casualty. The Dornier also had a disappointing bomb load of just over 2,000 pounds — less than half of its two other Luftwaffe con-temporaries (Heinkel 111 and Junkers 88). In fact, by the time World War II broke out, it was already obsolete.

The Dornier best illustrated the clandestine build-up of the German air force in the early 1930s. Built by Claudius Dornier's *Dorniere-Werke* factory, the specifications called for a passenger capacity of eight and space for carrying mail. But by the time it was delivered to Lufthansa, it was obvious to even the most uninitiated that this was no passenger plane. With some effort four people could be crammed into the so-called passenger space although there was certainly plenty of room in the mail compartment. A case of turning "ploughshares back into swords" instead of vice versa. To complete the deception, the airline's chief test pilot, Flukapitan Untucht, refused to accept the machine but heartily recommended that it be modified as a high-speed dash bomber.

The final chapter to this chicanery in the Dornier saga was written in July 1937 in the skies over Zurich at the International Military Aircraft Competition to demonstrate that Hitler's boast that the Luftwaffe had reached parity with Britain was not mere braggadocio, but a proven fact. It wasn't; it was a charade. The Dornier that caused such a sensation by flying at a speed of twenty-five miles an hour faster than the British biplanes then in service had two souped-up 600-hp BMW engines and had been stripped of all armament and unnecessary weight.

By the time it flew in the Battle of Britain, the Dornier's armament amounted to eight 7.9mm machine-guns. But it wasn't sufficient to protect it from the attacking fighters, so to try and shake them off the crews resorted to throwing out stick grenades in their wake. The powerplants consisted of two 1,000-hp Bramo radial air-cooled engines which gave the bomber a top speed of only 264 miles an hour.

Skeets Ogilvie, Spitfire pilot with 603 Squadron, topped the list of Canadian Do 17 scorers by shooting down two of them, one on each of two consecutive days.

*Dornier 17*

## DORNIER 215

The DO 215 was pretty well a carbon copy of the 17 but with two 1,150-hp Daimler-Benz liquid-cooled in-line engines, its maximum speed was improved by ten miles an hour. In addition to the standard armament, it was fitted with camera equipment and was chiefly used in a reconnaissance role. But, although there were fewer of them flown in the battle than their counterparts, Canadians posted higher scores against the Do 215 than the Do 17.

Ernie McNab, CO of No. 1 Squadron RCAF, led the parade by destroying two of them. The first one he destroyed made him the first RCAF pilot to shoot down an enemy plane in the Battle of Britain. Altogether twenty Canadian pilots, all but one them flying Hurricanes (the other a Spitfire pilot), accounted for nine Do 215s shot down, two probably destroyed, and twelve damaged. In addition, they also shared in the destruction of five others, two probably destroyed, and five damaged.

## HEINKEL 111

The success of the Canadians against Germany's first mass-produced bomber, destroying four and probably shooting down five plus damaging five more, was chiefly due to its vulnerability to head-on attack. For the same reason, seven pilots from the Dominion also shared in the demise of eight others.

Designed by the Gunther brothers, Walther and Siegfried, the He 111 was the Luftwaffe's largest twin-engine bomber and was typical of Ernst Heinkel's penchant for smooth lines, flush finishes and elliptically shaped wings (though in this case they were later modified to straighter, tapered mainplanes). But the most notable feature of the low-winged monoplane, built by his *Ernst Heinkel Flugzwerke* plant, was the enormous amount of glazing used in its nose. While this provided marvellous visibility for the forward members of the crew, it also rendered the aircraft dangerously open to frontal fire.

The Heinkel was another example of the surreptitious means employed by the Germans to furnish their covert air arm. Originally designed as a ten-passenger airliner, it could easily be converted to a medium bomber with a hefty payload of 4,000 pounds. But the Germans had seriously overrated its performance in combat. In Spain, like the Dornier, it was soon evident that the aircraft shouldn't fly without fighter protection. In the Battle of Britain, even fighter escort wasn't enough. Equipped with two 1,100-hp Daimler-Benz liquid-cooled engines, it could muster a top speed of only 255 to 275 miles an hour. Its five free-mounted 7.9mm machine-guns (later one of them was replaced with a 20mm cannon) proved so inadequate that the crews resorted to throwing out tin boxes attached to reels of wire in the hope of snagging an attacking fighter's propeller. At the height of the Battle of Britain in mid-September 1940, the He 111 had passed its prime as a day-bomber and was relegated to night raids. Later it was used for anti-shipping as well as transport work.

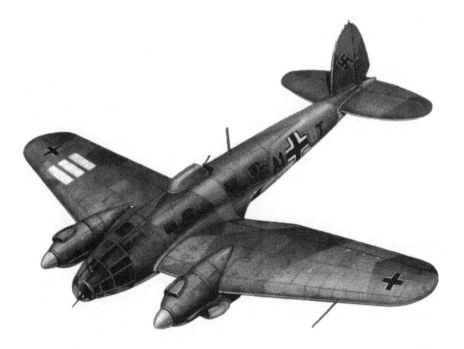

*Heinkel 111*

## HEINKEL 115

But for a chance encounter with a Blenheim flown by Andrew Fletcher on August 3, 1940, the Heinkel 115 float plane would never have formed part of the history of Canadians in the Battle of Britain, albeit a small, though honourable, mention. Initially conceived as a torpedo plane, in practice the Heinkel 115 was used for coastal reconnaissance and mine-laying, and was considered the best seaplane produced in World War

II. It was a fair match for the Blenheim. Armed with two machine-guns, it was a large aircraft with a wingspan of seventy-two feet and an overall length of sixty feet. Equipped with two 960-hp air-cooled BMW engines, it had a top speed of 220 miles an hour. In its ensuing exchange of unpleasantries with the Blenheim, it escaped leaving Fletcher credited with a damaged.

## HAWKER HURRICANE

More than seventy Canadians flew Hurricanes in the Battle of Britain, accounting for nearly 200 victories over the Germans in enemy aircraft shot down, probably destroyed and damaged — a ratio of three to one. Casualties amounted to just over 30 percent with nineteen pilots killed and eight wounded, one of whom later died of injuries. These losses might have been higher had it not been for the Hurricane's traditional fuselage construction of wood and fabric stiffened by a metal-tube framework which was much more resistant to exploding cannon shells that burst on contact than a metal finish. (The wings, however, were metal.) It had another advantage: improvised repairs could be carried out right on the station, minimizing the time an aircraft would be taken out of service.

The doughty warhorse had its origin when, in 1931, the British Air Ministry issued a specification to the leading airplane manufacturers for a fighter to replace the Bristol Bulldog biplane. Sydney Camm, chief designer for Hawker Aircraft Limited, submitted two plans, one for a monoplane, and another for a biplane. Both were rejected on the grounds that they were "too orthodox even for the Air Ministry."

In the meantime, Camm had learned of the new twelve-cylinder, 1,000-hp double-banked V-shaped engine under development at the Rolls-Royce Company (which later became the legendary Merlin). Camm proceeded to create a fighter based on its potential as a private venture without government subsidy. In substance it was a monoplane version of his earlier Fury biplane. He had nearly completed its design when the Air Ministry opened a new tender calling for a fighter to be mounted with either six or eight machine-guns. This decision to increase armament from the standard two or four guns represented a major breakthrough. It stemmed from a theory advanced by the head of the Air Ministry's Operational Requirements section, Ralph Sorley. With the increase in speeds he calculated that the average pilot could only hold a target in his sights for two seconds at most. The fire brought to bear therefore had to be especially lethal.

This hypothesis was accepted and at the same time the more rapid-firing Browning machine-gun replaced the reliable old stand-by from WWI, the Vickers. Camm comfortably accommodated this fresh requirement by simply modifying the wings to install the eight guns so that, in no time at all, by November 6, 1935, the Hurricane flew for the first time.

Although it was only a prototype demonstration, the significance to this unheralded event was that Britain at last had a modern-day fighter in the air. Call it an interim stop-gap between the canvas biplanes and the all-metal monoplanes, it nonetheless filled the breach created by the emergence of the German Dornier and Heinkel bombers and Messerschmitt 109 fighter prototypes already in flight. The British were at least starting to catch up, and by the beginning of World War II they had 497 Hurricanes on the line with eighteen squadrons so equipped.

The Hurricanes flown by Canadians in the Battle of Britain were the Marks I and II, fitted with three-blade propellers and powered by 1,030 and 1,185-hp Merlin engines, giving them top speeds of between 325 and 342 miles an hour. A delight to fly, they took off and landed with ease. Their most important characteristics in combat were a tight turning radius and a rapid rate of climb of up to 2,420 feet a minute.

Four Canadian Hurricane pilots qualified as aces, the top scorer being Willie McKnight of 242 Squadron who destroyed six aircraft and shared in the destruction of another. Joe Laricheliere, with 213 Squadron, ran a close second with six planes shot down. The other two were both RCAF pilots: Gordie McGregor with five destroyed, two probables, and five damaged to his credit; and Ernie McNab with a score of five destroyed, one probable, as well as three damaged and a share in damaging another.

*Hawker Hurricane*

## JUNKERS 87

In Spain, Poland, Norway and Western Europe, the Ju 87 *Stuka*, an abbreviation of *Sturkampfflugzeug* (literally meaning "plunge-battle air-craft"), paved the way for the invading German Panzer divisions as long-range aerial artillery, terrorizing ground troops and civilian refugees by diving to ground level with guns blazing and sirens wailing and scattering bombs at will. But in the Battle of Britain, it scared no one. In fact it proved so hopelessly inadequate against a proper air defence that it had to be withdrawn. In mid-August 1940, three Canadians shared in that demise.

Its impotency in the battle was one thing, but more significant to the outcome of that struggle was the impact its very existence made on the shape and conduct of the Luftwaffe itself. In 1929, on a visit to the United States, Ernst Udet, Germany's second ranking WWI ace, tested a Curtiss Hawk, a US Navy carrier-borne dive-bomber. He became so mesmerized with the aircraft and the dive-bombing concept that he brought one back to Germany and demonstrated it to Goering and en-tourage who were enchanted by the notion. This was to have fatal re-percussions and consequences for the Luftwaffe.

Although there were sceptics who knew that it was suicidal to expose a slow-flying bomber to high-speed fighters, not to mention ground-fire under 3,000 feet, the prevailing feeling remained that the *Stuka* would be the prime long-range artillery weapon of the next war. But it was short-range thinking by an air force hierarchy that was short-range minded. One person who strongly opposed this view might just have been able to dissuade the German Air Ministry from building its hopes on dive-bombers — had he lived long enough.

Walther Wever, the Luftwaffe's first chief of staff, believed that while

*Junkers 87*

tactical bombing could win battles, only strategic bombing could win a war. That meant penetrating far behind frontiers which called for long-range four-engine bombers. His focus was on Russia — "the real enemy" — not Britain and France. The strategic targets were distant beyond the Ural mountains. Before he was killed in a plane crash in 1936, on his authorization Dornier had already built a prototype known as the "Ural" bomber. But after Wever's death, Goering scuttled the aircraft and, along with it, any and all strategic possibilities it portended.

When the Ju 87, built by *Junkers Fluzeuge und Motorenwerke*, went into service in 1937, the Luftwaffe hierarchy became so enamoured with the dive-bombing concept that orders were issued that forthwith all new aircraft designs were to incorporate a dive-bombing capability. In one case the time needed to make these modifications seriously slowed production.

After being withdrawn from the Battle of Britain, the *Stuka* was never again used in such a role. Its sphere was limited to close-army support in Africa, Greece and Russia.

The three Canadians who scored against the Ju 87 were Pete Gordon of Red Deer who damaged one on August 11, Harry Mitchell from Port Hope who shot one down on August 14, and Joe Laricheliere of Montreal who destroyed one on the following day. All three were Hurricane pilots flying with the RAF.

## JUNKERS 88

The Ju 88 was the Luftwaffe's only satisfactory bomber. It was the most versatile aircraft the Germans produced although it was still no match for the Hurricanes and Spitfires. All told, Canadians ran up a tally of seven 88s destroyed, two probably destroyed and six damaged, as well as sharing in six shot down, one probably destroyed and another damaged.

Designed as a medium bomber to accommodate a crew of three, later increased to four, it was the only craft that did not go through a phase where it was manufactured to be an airliner to begin with. And it certainly never resembled one. Typical of Hugo Junkers, aircraft designs, it was brutish, rugged and robust.

Launched in June 1936 by Wilhelm Evers and Alfred Gassner of *Junkers Flugzeuge und Motorenwerke*, it flew on December 2 that year and performed so satisfactorily that manufacturing was assigned a Class 1 priority. Dr. Heinrich Kopenberg, directing the operation, was assigned a free hand to raid the other manufacturers for material as well as personnel such as engineers. He was also allowed to subcontract parts and technology to Junkers' competitors.

Despite the carte blanche and the high-handed methods used to employ them, production struck a snag when Hans Jeschonneck took over as Luftwaffe chief of staff. Convinced by Udet that dive-bombing should be given precedence over everything else, he ordered this capability incorporated into all bombers under construction which included the Ju 88. This called for such drastic modifications as installing dive-breaks; these and other changes slowed manufacture to the extent that the Ju 88 was still in the pre-batch production stage when WWII broke out.

By the time it flew in the Battle of Britain, the thrust from its two 1,200-hp Jumo (another of Junkers' enterprises) liquid-cooled in-line engines, housed in radial cowlings, gave the Ju 88 a top speed of 268 miles an hour. Armament consisted of four machine-guns, and it had a bomb load of 4,000 pounds carried externally with a small load inside.

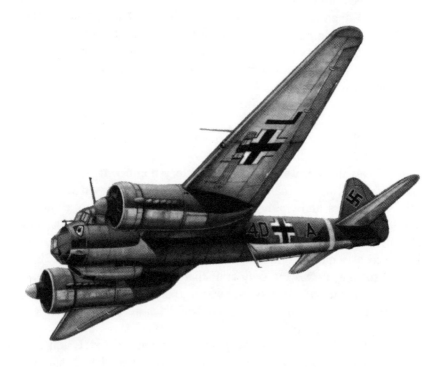

*Junkers 88*

## MESSERSCHMITT 109

Canadian pilots made their heaviest score in the Battle of Britain against the German fighter that shot down more aircraft in the entire war than any other on either side. Forty-three-and-a-half Messerschmitt 109s fell to their guns, another ten were probably destroyed, and sixteen were damaged. Twenty-eight Hurricane and three Spitfire pilots figured in the scoring. Quite a record against a rugged opponent.

Vis-à-vis speed, the Hurricane was at a slight disadvantage though the Spitfire was evenly matched. The same applied to rate of climb. Where the Me 109 held the edge was in its higher-altitude and faster zoom ability — from a dive into a climb — and its direct fuel-injection system. A 109 pilot could suddenly plunge his fighter down at any speed from any angle by simply pushing the control column forward no matter how harshly, without choking the engine, as was the case with the RAF fighters whose motors conked out from the same manoeuvre. Where the Messerschmitt was at a decided disadvantage against the Hurricane or the Spitfire was its inability to hold either one of them in a turn. By the same token, both of them could easily turn inside the 109. Its most serious flaw, however, was its inability to withstand much battle damage due to its light structure. But it was still a tough old bird by any standard.

Its evolution was as cantankerous as its erratic, irascible designer, Willy Messerschmitt, technical director of *Bayerische Fluzeuge Werke* (BFW), whose relations with the Nazi Party were ambiguous to say the least. Erhard Milch, head of the Air Ministry, disliked and distrusted him. One of his closest friends had been killed in one of Messerschmitt's airplanes. As a result, BFW was excluded from contracts with the German government. In defiance, Messerschmitt sold his planes to Rumania, a step that heightened the hostility between the two men. Milch passed the word around the Luftwaffe that BFW planes were unreliable and

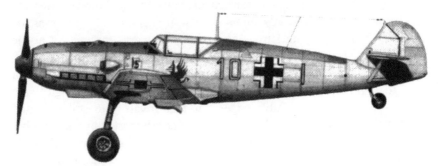

*Messerschmitt 109*

unsafe. But Messerschmitt had an undying ally and supporter in the Nazi Deputy Fuehrer, Rudolf Hess, who became captivated with the Bf 108 *Taifun*, a single-engine, low-wing monoplane. An all-metal four-passenger touring plane, with retractable landing gear, it had Handley-Page automatic slats attached to the leading edge of the wings to prevent it from stalling, making it as safe as any plane could be. When tenders were issued to the aircraft manufacturers in 1934 for a new, modern fighter for the Luftwaffe, Hess ordered Wilhelm Wimmer, in charge of new aircraft at the Air Ministry's Technical Office, to make sure BFW was on the list.

Messerschmitt proceeded to narrow the Bf 108 into a single-seat fighter. During its development the BFW name was changed to *Messerschmitt*, and although the new fighter was officially designated the Bf 109, it was commonly known as the Me 109. Of flush-riveted, all-metal construction, its wings were small and square-tipped which gave it a very high wing loading. For that reason Messerschmitt retained the Handley-Page slats he had fitted to the Bf 108. It had its faults. The Me 109's cockpit canopy was slab-sided on the right and opened sideways. It was awkward and visibility was limited. The narrow, outwardly splayed undercarriage gave the aircraft a tendency to ground-loop — swing sharply to one side and buckle a wheel — on both take-off and landing, which was particularly pronounced in a crosswind.

But at the Travemunde fighter trials in September 1935, the Messerschmitt, the only fighter with an enclosed cockpit, won hands down over the competition and immediately went into production. Its next test was the real thing, in battle. During the Spanish Civil War, it gave a good account of itself, but was no match for the Russian-built *Polikarpov* I-16, known as the "Mosca." Nevertheless, the experience under actual combat conditions, revealing weaknesses that would not otherwise have been so readily apparent, proved invaluable.

The most important lesson learned in that conflict, however, was the development by the Me 109 pilots of new fighter tactics. Shedding the WWI Richthofen Flying Circus formation which was impractical at the new high speeds, they adopted the *Schwarm*, two pairs (*Rottes*) of aircraft, spaced well apart allowing for maximum flexibility and permitting each pilot to guard his partner's rear. In the Battle of Britain, it gave the Me 109 pilots a considerable edge over their rivals who still practised the Vic formation — fine for air shows and fly-pasts, but in combat only the leader could search the sky; his wingmen on either side were too busy keeping formation. It was almost a year after the battle ended before the Allied air forces switched to the "finger four" formation which took the *Schwarm* a step further. It allowed four pilots in a section, spread out like the fingers of a hand, to cover each other's tail.

The Messerschmitt 109 that flew in the Battle was the model "E" which its pilots nicknamed the "Emil." It had a 1,100-hp Daimler-Benz engine that delivered a maximum speed of 345 miles an hour. In the initial stages it was extraordinarily vulnerable because the fuel tank sat behind the pilot. Later, armour plating was installed for protection. Armament consisted of two machine-guns mounted in the engine cowling and two 20mm cannon in the wings. Half a dozen cannon shells could do far more damage than the equivalent burst from the Hurricane or Spitfire's Brownings. But the rate of fire of the machine-guns was higher which provided a better chance of scoring with a short burst. Towards the end of the Battle the Emil was also used as a fighter-bomber. A modified version could outperform the Spitfire over 20,000 feet.

Its chief limitations were that there were not enough Me 109s available, and its limited range of only 412 miles and limited endurance due to the unavailability of drop tanks allowed the Me 109 a mere twenty minutes' combat time.

The leading Canadian scorers against the 109s were John Boyle from Casselman and Bill Nelson of Montreal — both Spitfire pilots — and Lionel Gaunce from Lethbridge who flew Hurricanes. Each had four Emils to his credit. Gaunce also damaged a 109.


## MESSERSCHMITT 110

Goering's idea! Captivated by the success of two-seater planes during WWI, he decided to form an élite strategic force of *Zerstorerstaffeln* (destroyer squadrons) equipped with long-range fighters manned by hand-picked aircrews. Not a bad concept, really. But it was doomed to failure from the outset.

In the first place, after Walther Wever, Germany's proponent of a strategic air force, was killed and the four-engine bomber abandoned, with its emphasis on dive-bombing and tactical medium bombers the Luftwaffe never stood a chance of becoming anything close to resembling a strategic air force. And in the Battle of Britain the twin-engine Messerschmitt 110 *Zerstorers*, with their poor acceleration and wide turning radius, were no match for the British fighters. In fact, they proved to be so pitifully awkward and defenceless that they had to be escorted by Me 109s.

As an example, Canadians scored their second-highest successes against the 110 — twenty-four destroyed, three probably shot down and fourteen damaged as well as sharing in destroying and probably destroying four more. Willie McKnight of Edmonton led his countrymen by shooting down three of the *Zerstorers*.

First flown in May 1936, the Me 110 was plagued with production problems from the start and never got into mass manufacture until mid-1939. It carried a crew of two, sometimes three, and was armed with four fixed machine-guns and two 20mm cannon as well as one swivel gun. Its two 1,150-hp twelve-cylinder liquid-cooled in-line Daimler-Benz engines gave it a top speed of 340 miles an hour. In fairness, although it fared poorly in the battle, if the 110 had a chance to attack from a high level for a single pass before breaking away, it could be quite effective.

The Me 110 was later assigned to dive-bombing, reconnaissance and, where it succeeded best, night-fighting. By 1944, sixty percent of the Luftwaffe night-fighter force was made up of Me 110s.

*Messerschmitt 110*

## SUPERMARINE SPITFIRE

Only fourteen Canadians flew Spitfires in the Battle of Britain, but their average hit record of four enemy planes per pilot — twenty-two destroyed, eight probably shot down, eleven damaged and a share in the doom of seven others — was notable. More significant, however, is the fact that more Spitfires became operational with the RCAF during WWII than any other warplane; thirteen fighter and fighter-reconnaissance squadrons were fortified with them. And this did not take into account the Canadians who flew the fighter with RAF squadrons.

With its graceful elliptical wings, smooth rounded lines, and performance par excellence, the Spitfire still stands as the classic fighter of all time. But it might never have got off the ground or, even onto the drawing board, had it not been for the generosity of an eccentric widow of a millionaire shipping magnate.

In 1929, the British won the biannual Schneider Trophy seaplane race for the second time in a row. A third victory would capture the coveted prize for which the major nations had been competing since 1913. But for Great Britain, there was more at stake here than just a trophy. The S6 racer powered by a Rolls-Royce engine, designed by Reginald "RJ" Mitchell, and built by the Supermarine Division of Vickers-Armstrong Ltd., was destined to become the ancestor of the Spitfire. In the meantime, economics and politics played a heavy hand.

Up until the mid-1920s, the aircraft manufacturers could afford to sustain the cost of building the racers provided the military supplied the pilots to fly them. But the swift technological progress of aviation soon put the price out of reach of the private sector. Because international prestige was involved, the governments then agreed to underwrite the expenses. Then, in 1931, the British Cabinet under Ramsay MacDonald cut all further subsidies on the grounds that the country was in the middle of a financial crisis.

Lady Lucy Houston to the rescue. "To prevent the Socialists from being spoil sports" whom she said "made my blood boil," she volunteered to provide the necessary funds needed for Britain to enter the race. At midday on Sunday, September 13, 1931, John Boothman of the RAF won the trophy outright for England in the S6B, completing the triangular Spithead course at an average speed of 340.08 miles an hour, and establishing a new world speed record. Although a lot of rough air lay ahead, the emergence of the Spitfire was assured. This was to be of paramount consequence to the Royal Canadian Air Force as we have seen.

In the fall of the year that the British won the Schneider Trophy, the Air Ministry issued a specification for a fighter to replace the British

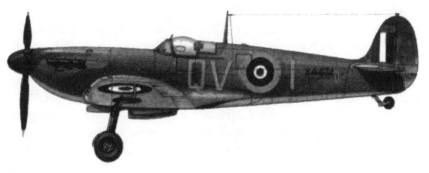

*Spitfire*

Bulldog biplane. This was Mitchell's first attempt at landplane fighter design and based on their experience with the high-speed winning seaplanes, he and his design team thought it would be a breeze. They soon learned differently. The Supermarine entry was a monstrosity. A low-wing monoplane with cranked mainplanes, it had a fixed undercarriage covered by spats, and was equipped with a 660-hp Rolls-Royce Goshawk engine capable of 238 miles an hour. To no one's surprise (even Mitchell's), along with seven others it lost out to the Gloster Gladiator biplane.

Even though he was dying of cancer, Mitchell refused to be deterred. He decided to stick with his design and modify it. Now the genesis of the Spitfire began to take shape. Early revisions called for clean straight tapered wings and an enclosed cockpit. Still, the Air Ministry remained lukewarm. Despite this bureaucratic indifference, however, the Supermarine board voted to proceed with its construction as a private venture. Shortly afterwards, Supermarine and Rolls-Royce reached an agreement that the new fighter would incorporate the latter's new 1,000-hp engine, later named the Merlin. Now Mitchell visualized speeds of over 300 miles an hour where the ultimate in streamlining would be essential. For that reason he decided his fighter would be of all-metal construction and he was determined to incorporate as many of the lessons learned designing the record-breaking "S" racers.

These developments drew fresh interest from the Air Ministry which, on December 1, 1934, issued a contract providing £10,000 to go towards Mitchell's "improved" design. The private venture had lasted less than a month. During discussions with Ralph Sorley, in charge of operational requirements at the Air Ministry, Mitchell agreed that he could install eight Browning machine-guns in the new machine. This led to the elliptical wing, the hallmark of the Spitfire, but not for aesthetic reasons. That was a bonus. The choice was made for much more practical purposes. Aerodynamically, the ellipse shape was the best solution to housing the guns and the outwardly retracting wheels and still making the wings as thin and strong as possible.

The Spitfire's sleek flush finish resulted from a visit made by one of the members of the design team, Beverley Shenston, to the Paris Aero Show. There the Toronto-born engineer had become fascinated with the finish on the Heinkel 70 passenger plane. It was so smooth that, without Mitchell's knowledge, he wrote to Ernst Heinkel asking whether it was metal or wood. Back came a reply that the skinning was metal with sunken rivets. Thus a potential adversary had provided a future antagonist with a valuable tip on how to produce more speed to attack the bomber he was producing. Another innovation to the Spitfire was the introduction of "oleo" legs. A pneumatic, telescoping combination of oil and air provided a spring-like action that cushioned the impact of heavy and bumpy landings.

Designing the Spitfire was not a task to be hurried. It required patience; Mitchell wanted the "best fighter in the world." By the summer of 1935, it was complete but only on the drawing board and as a wooden mock-up. It took until February of the following year to finish the construction of the prototype, which took to the air for the first time on March 6, 1936.

That virgin flight was so smooth and free of vices that, on alighting from the cockpit, test pilot Mutt Summers said to Mitchell: "Don't change a thing. It's perfect."

By this time, the Supermarine executive had already christened the machine "Spitfire," a name that will ever remain synonymous with fighter aircraft and the Battle of Britain in particular. But when Mitchell, a man with an impish sense of humour, learned of it, he quipped: "Just the sort of bloody silly name they would give it."

After further testing and nitty-gritty alterations and modifications, in June 1936 the Air Ministry accepted it and placed an initial order for 310 to be built. Up to that time its development had cost the British taxpayer £15,776 to produce a fighter that played a key role in defeating what seemed to be an invincible enemy. To paraphrase once more — rarely has so little been invested to achieve so much.

Tragically, Mitchell never lived to see a production model of his winged legacy to the free world in flight. Throughout its development his health deteriorated steadily. A lesser person would have packed it in. But Mitchell had visited Germany where he had been witness to the growing Nazi military might and was resolutely determined to see his fighter built.

At the beginning of the Battle of Britain, the RAF had nineteen Spitfire squadrons, all of which were equipped with the Mark 1. Fitted with a two-blade propeller, its 1,030-hp Merlin engine gave it a maximum speed of 355 miles an hour and a rate of climb of 9.4 minutes to 20,000 feet. The Mark II, which reached the squadrons in the later stages of the battle, had a three-blade airscrew and could reach a top speed of 370 miles an hour and had an improved rate of climb of 2,600 feet a minute.

Canadians had one Spitfire ace in the Battle, Bill Nelson from Montreal, who had been awarded the DFC as a bomber pilot before transferring to fighters with 74 Squadron. Nelson destroyed five enemy aircraft and damaged two others. Ironically he was killed on November 1, 1940, the day after the battle ended.

# II/THE SPLENDID HUNDRED BOX-SCORE*

| | Squadron | Flying | Destroyed | Probably Destroyed | Damaged |
|---|---|---|---|---|---|
| Arthur, Charles Ian<br>P/O<br>Winnipeg, Man. | 141<br>Hawkinge | Defiants | 0 | 0 | 0 |
| Barton, Richard Alexander "Butch"<br>F/L<br>Kamloops, B.C.<br>*Awarded DFC October 22* | 249<br>North Weald | Hurricanes | 3 1/2 | 2 1/2 | 4 |
| Beardmore, Eric<br>F/O<br>Montreal, P.Q.<br>*Wounded September 18* | 1 RCAF<br>Northolt | Hurricanes | 0 | 0 | 0 |
| Beley, Robert Wilfred<br>P/O<br>Rossland, B.C.<br>*Died of wounds August 12* | 151<br>Digby | Hurricanes | 0 | 0 | 0 |

*All data 1940 unless otherwise posted.

| | Squadron | Flying | Destroyed | Probably Destroyed | Damaged |
|---|---|---|---|---|---|
| Beake, Percival Harold<br>P/O<br>Quebec, P.Q. | 64<br>Church Fenton | Spitfires | 0 | 0 | 0 |
| Benzie, John<br>P/O<br>Winnipeg, Man.<br>*Killed in action September 7* | 242<br>Coltishall | Hurricanes | 0 | 0 | 0 |
| Blatchford, Harold Peter "Cowboy"<br>F/L<br>Edmonton, Alta.<br>*Awarded DFC December 5, 1940*<br>*First Canadian in the RAF to*<br>*command an RCAF wing* | 17 & 257<br>Catterick & Debden | Spitfires & Hurricanes | ½/½ | 0 | 0 |
| Bonseigneur, Camille<br>P/O<br>Regina, Sask.<br>*Killed in action September 3* | 257<br>Debden | Hurricanes | 1/2 | 0 | 0 |
| Boyle, John Grier<br>P/O<br>Casselman, Ont.<br>*Killed in action September 22* | 41<br>Hornchurch | Spitfires | 4 1/5 | 0 | 0 |

| | | | | | | |
|---|---|---|---|---|---|---|
| Briese, Charles<br>F/O<br>Rosetown, Sask. | 1 RCAF<br>Northolt | Hurricanes | 0 | 0 | 0 | |
| Brown, Edward de Pyster<br>"DePyster"<br>F/O<br>Coronado, Calif. | 1 RCAF<br>Northolt | Hurricanes | 1 | 0 | 0 | |
| Brown, Mark Kenry<br>"Hilly"<br>F/L<br>Portage la Prairie, Man. | 1 RAF<br>Northolt & Wittering | Hurricanes | 1 1/2 | 0 | 0 | |
| Brown, Marvin Kitchener<br>P/O<br>Kincardine, Ont. | 242<br>Coltishall | Hurricanes | 0 | 0 | 0 | |
| Bryson, John<br>"Johnny"<br>P/O<br>Montreal, P.Q.<br>*Killed in action September 24* | 92<br>Biggin Hill | Spitfires | 0 | 0 | 0 | |
| Campbell, Norman Neil<br>P/O<br>St. Thomas, Ont.<br>*Killed in action October 17* | 242<br>Coltishall | Hurricanes | 2 | 0 | 2 | |

| | Squadron | Flying | Destroyed | Probably Destroyed | Damaged |
|---|---|---|---|---|---|
| Carriere, Joseph Charles P/O Quebec, P.Q. | 219 Catterick | Blenheims | 0 | 0 | 0 |
| Carthew, George P/O Mountain Park, Alta. | 253 Kenley | Hurricanes | 0 | 0 | 0 |
| Carpenter, John Conway "Jack" Sub-Lt (RN) Toronto, Ont. *Seconded from the Royal Navy to the Royal Air Force Killed in action September 8* | 222 & 46 Hornchurch & North Weald | Hurricanes | 2 | 0 | 0 |
| Cave, John Geoffery P/O Calgary, Alta. | 242 Coltishall | Hurricanes | 0 | 0 | 0 |
| Charles, Edward Francis John "Jack" P/O & F/O Lashburn, Sask. | 54 Catterick | Spitfires | 0 | 0 | 0 |
| Chevrier, John P/O St. Lambert, P.Q. | 1 RCAF Northolt | Hurricanes | 0 | 0 | 0 |

| Name | Rank | Hometown | Squadron | Aircraft | | | |
|---|---|---|---|---|---|---|---|
| Christie, George | F/O | Westmount, P.Q. | 242 Coltishall | Hurricanes | 0 | 0 | 0 |
| Christmas, Beverley "Bev" | F/O | St. Hilaire, P.Q. | 1 RCAF Northolt | Hurricanes | 2 | 0 | 5/6 |
| Cochrane, Arthur Charles "Jimmy" | P/O | Vernon, B.C. | 257 Debden | Hurricanes | 4 | 1 | 2 |
| Corbett, George Henry | P/O | Victoria, B.C. | 66 Biggin Hill | Spitfires | 1 | 0 | 1 |
| Corbett, Vaughan | F/L | Westmount, P.Q. | 1 RCAF Northolt | Hurricanes | 0 | 0 | 1 |
| Cryderman, Lawrence Elwood "Larry" | P/O | Toronto, Ont. | 242 Coltishall | Hurricanes | 0 | 0 | 0 |
| Desloges, Jean-Paul John Joseph "Paul" | F/O | Ottawa, Ont. | 1 RCAF Northolt | Hurricanes | 0 | 0 | 0 |

| | Squadron | Flying | Destroyed | Probably Destroyed | Damaged |
|---|---|---|---|---|---|
| Dibnah, Robert Harold<br>P/O<br>Winnipeg, Man. | 1 & 242<br>Northolt & Coltishall | Hurricanes | 1 | 0 | 1 |
| Edwards, Harold Davis<br>"Harry"<br>P/O<br>Winnipeg, Man.<br>*Killed in action September 11* | 92<br>Biggin Hill | Spitfires | 1/2 | 0 | 0 |
| Edwards, Robert<br>"Bob"<br>F/O<br>Cobourg, Ont.<br>*Killed in action August 26* | 1 RCAF<br>Northolt | Hurricanes | 1 | 0 | 0 |
| Edy, Alan Laird<br>P/O<br>Winnipeg, Man. | 602<br>Tangmere | Spitfires | 1 | 1 | 1/7 |
| Elliott, George James<br>Winnipeg, Man.<br>*Member of the RCAF attached to the RAF* | 607<br>Tangmere | Hurricanes | 0 | 0 | 0 |
| Edmond, Norman Douglas<br>P/O<br>Calgary, Alta. | 615<br>Northolt | Hurricanes | 0 | 0 | 0 |

| Name | Squadron | Base | Aircraft | | | |
|---|---|---|---|---|---|---|
| Fiske, William "Bill" P/O Montreal, P.Q. *Died of wounds August 17* | 601 | Filton | Hurricanes | 1 | 0 | 0 |
| Fletcher, Andrew William F/L Lethbridge, Alta. *Awarded DFC October 26* | 23 | Tangmere | Blenheims | 2 | 0 | 1 |
| Fumerton, Robert Carl "Moose" F/L Fort Cologne, P.Q. | 32 | Acklington | Hurricanes | 0 | 0 | 0 |
| Gaunce, Lionel Manly F/L & S/L Lethbridge, Alta. | 615 & 46 | Northolt & North Weald | Hurricanes | 4 | 1 | 1 |
| Gordon, John Arthur "Pete" S/L Red Deer, Alta. | 151 | Digby | Hurricanes | 1 | 0 | 1 |
| Grassick, Robert Davidson "Slim" P/O London, Ont. | 242 | Coltishall | Hurricanes | 0 | 0 | 0 |

| | Squadron | Flying | Destroyed | Probably Destroyed | Damaged |
|---|---|---|---|---|---|
| Hamilton, Harold "Hammy" F/L Oak Point, N.B. *Killed in action August 29* | 85 Church Fenton | Hurricanes | 2 1/2 | 1 | 1 |
| Harnett, Thomas Patrick "Tom" F/O Moncton, N.B. | 219 Catterick | Blenheims | 0 | 0 | 0 |
| Hart, John Stuart P/O Sackville, N.B. | 54 & 602 Catterick & Tangmere | Spitfires | 1 | 1/3 | 0 |
| Hart, Norris "Norrie" P/O Dugald, Man. *Killed in action November 5* | 242 Coltishall | Hurricanes | 4 | 0 | 0 |
| Hewitt, Duncan Alexander P/O Saint John, N.B. *Killed in action July 12* | 501 Kenley | Hurricanes | 0 | 0 | 0 |
| Hillock, Frank Toronto, Ont. | 1 RCAF Northolt | Hurricanes | 0 | 0 | 0 |

| Pilot | Squadron/Base | Aircraft | | | |
|---|---|---|---|---|---|
| Howley, Alexander "Alex" P/O Victoria, B.C. *Killed in action July 19* | 141 Hawkinge | Defiants | 0 | 0 | 0 |
| Hyde, George F/O Westmount, P.Q. *Wounded August 31* | 1 RCAF Northolt | Hurricanes | 0 | 0 | 0 |
| Johnston, James "Swede" P/O Brandon, Man. *Killed in action August 15* | 151 Digby | Hurricanes | 0 | 0 | 0 |
| Kent, John "Johnny" F/L Winnipeg, Man. *Awarded DFC October 25* | 303 (Polish) Northolt | Hurricanes | 4 | 1 | 2 |
| Kerwin, John F/O Toronto, Ont. | 1 RCAF Northolt | Hurricanes | 2 | 0 | 1 |

| Name | Squadron | Flying | Destroyed | Probably Destroyed | Damaged |
|---|---|---|---|---|---|
| Laricheliere, Joseph "Joe" P/O Montreal, P.Q. *Killed in action August 16* | 213 Tangmere | Hurricanes | 6 | 0 | 0 |
| Latta, John Blandford P/O Vancouver, B.C. | 242 Coltishall | Hurricanes | 4 1/3 | 0 | 0 |
| Lawrence, Kenneth Aubyn Halifax, N.S. & Ottawa, Ont. | 234 & 603 St. Eval & Hornchurch | Spitfires | 2 1/3 | 1 | 5 |
| Lewis, Richard F/O Vancouver, B.C. | 1 RAF Northolt & Wittering | Hurricanes | 1 | 0 | 0 |
| Little, Thomas "Tommy" F/O Montreal, P.Q. | 1 RCAF Northolt | Hurricanes | 1 | 0 | 1 1/3 |
| Lochnan, Peter "Pete" F/O Ottawa, Ont. | 1 RCAF Northolt | Hurricanes | 1 2/3 | 0 | 4 |

| | | | | | |
|---|---|---|---|---|---|
| MacDougall, Robert<br>S/L<br>Toronto, Ont. | 17<br>Debden | Hurricanes | 0 | 0 | 0 |
| McGregor, Roy Gordon<br>"Gordie"<br>Montreal, P.Q.<br>*Awarded DFC October 25; one of two RCAF pilots to be so decorated* | 1 RCAF<br>Northolt | Hurricanes | 5 | 2 | 5 |
| McKnight, William Lidstone<br>"Willie"<br>P/O<br>Edmonton, Alta.<br>*Awarded bar to DFC October 8* | 242<br>Coltishall | Hurricanes | 6 1/2 | 0 | 0 |
| McNab Ernest, Archibald<br>"Ernie"<br>S/L<br>Rosthern, Sask.<br>*Awarded DFC October 22; first RCAF pilot to be decorated* | 1 RCAF<br>Northolt | Hurricanes | 5 | 1 | 3 1/2 |
| Millar, William<br>"Bill"<br>F/O<br>Penticton, B.C.<br>*Wounded September 9* | 1 RCAF<br>Northolt | Hurricanes | 0 | 0 | 0 |

| | Squadron | Flying | Destroyed | Probably Destroyed | Damaged |
|---|---|---|---|---|---|
| Milne, John Archibald<br>P/O<br>Corklin, Sask.<br>*Wounded October 22* | 605<br>Kenley | Hurricanes | 1 | 0 | 0 |
| Mitchell, Harold Thomas<br>"Harry"<br>P/O<br>Port Hope, Ont.<br>*Awarded DFC February 11, 1941* | 87<br>Filton | Hurricanes | 3 | 0 | 1 |
| Molson, Hartland de Montarville<br>F/O<br>Montreal, P.Q.<br>*Wounded October 5* | 1 RCAF<br>Northolt | Hurricanes | 1 | 0 | 3 |
| Nelson, William Henry<br>"Bill"<br>F/O<br>*Killed in action November 1* | 74<br>Coltishall | Spitfires | 5 | 0 | 2 |
| Nesbitt, Arthur Deane<br>F/O<br>Westmount, P.Q.<br>*Wounded September 15* | 1 RCAF<br>Northolt | Hurricanes | 2 | 0 | 1 |
| Norris, Robert<br>F/O<br>Saskatoon, Sask. | 1 RCAF<br>Northolt | Hurricanes | 0 | 1 | 1 |

| Name | Squadron & Base | Aircraft | | | |
|---|---|---|---|---|---|
| O'Brian, Peter<br>F/L & S/L<br>Toronto, Ont. | 247 & 152<br>St. Eval & Middle Wallop | Gladiators and Spitfires | 5/6 | 1/3 | 0 |
| Ogilvie, Alfred Keith<br>"Skeets"<br>P/O<br>Ottawa, Ont. | 609<br>Middle Wallop | Spitfires | 3 | 3 | 2 |
| Pattison, John<br>F/O<br>Toronto, Ont. | 1 RCAF<br>Northolt | Hurricanes | 0 | 0 | 0 |
| Peterson, Otto John<br>F/O<br>Halifax, N.S.<br>*Killed in action September 27* | 1 RCAF<br>Northolt | Hurricanes | 1 1/2 | 1 | 3 |
| Pitcher, Paul Brooks<br>P/O<br>Montreal, P.Q.<br>*Mentioned in Dispatches* | 1 RCAF<br>Northolt | Hurricanes | 1 | 0 | 3 |
| Pollock, William<br>"Bill"<br>F/O<br>Montreal, P.Q. | 1 RCAF<br>Northolt | Hurricanes | 0 | 0 | 0 |
| Pushman, George Rupert<br>P/O<br>Ottawa, Ont. | 213<br>Tangmere | Hurricanes | 0 | 0 | 0 |

| | Squadron | Flying | Destroyed | Probably Destroyed | Damaged |
|---|---|---|---|---|---|
| Reilly, Hugh William<br>P/O<br>London, Ont.<br>*Killed in action October 17* | 66<br>Gravesend | Spitfires | 1 | 0 | 0 |
| Reyno, Edward<br>F/L<br>Halifax, N.S. | 1 RCAF<br>Northolt | Hurricanes | 0 | 0 | 1/3 |
| Russel, Blair Dalzell<br>"Dal"<br>F/O<br>Toronto, Ont.<br>*Awarded DFC October 25; one of two RCAF pilots to be so decorated* | 1 RCAF<br>Northolt | Hurricanes | 3 | 2 | 3 |
| Schlanders, Kirkpatrick Maclure<br>P/O<br>St. John's, Nfld.<br>*Killed in action September 9* | 242<br>Coltishall | Hurricanes | 0 | 0 | 0 |
| Seddon, John William<br>F/O<br>Vancouver, B.C. | 601<br>Filton | Hurricanes | 0 | 0 | 0 |
| Smith, Arthur William<br>P/O<br>Summerland, B.C. | 141<br>Hawkinge | Defiants | 0 | 0 | 0 |

| | | | | | |
|---|---|---|---|---|---|
| Smith, Forgrave Marshall "Hiram" F/L Edmonton, Alta. *Wounded August 30* | 72 Biggin Hill | Spitfires | 0 | 0 | 0 |
| Smith, James Duncan "Smudger" F/O Winnipeg, Man. | 73 Debden | Hurricanes | 2 | 0 | 1 |
| Smith, Robert Rutherford "Bob" F/O London, Ont. | 229 Northolt | Hurricanes | 0 | 0 | 0 |
| Smither, Ross F/O London, Ont. *Killed in action September 15* | 1 RCAF Northolt | Hurricanes | 1 | 0 | 2 |
| Sprague, Henry Arthur P/O Hamilton, Ont. *Member of RCAF attached to RAF* | 3 Wick | Hurricanes | 0 | 0 | 0 |
| Sprenger, William "Bill" F/O Montreal, P.Q. | 1 RCAF Northolt | Hurricanes | 0 | 0 | 0 |

| | Squadron | Flying | Destroyed | Probably Destroyed | Damaged |
|---|---|---|---|---|---|
| Stansfeld, Noel Karl<br>P/O<br>Edmonton, Alta. | 242 & 229<br>Coltishall & Northolt | Hurricanes | 2 5/6 | 1 | 1 |
| Tamblyn, Hugh Norman<br>P/O & F/O<br>Watrous, Sask.<br>*Awarded DFC January 7, 1941* | 141 & 242<br>Turnhouse & Coltishall | Defiants & Hurricanes | 4 1/2 | 1 | 1 |
| Trevena, Charles<br>F/O<br>Regina, Sask. | 1 RCAF<br>Northolt | Hurricanes | 0 | 0 | 0 |
| Trueman, Alexander Albert Craig<br>"Alex"<br>Toronto, Ont.<br>*Killed in action September 4* | 253<br>Kenley | Hurricanes | 0 | 0 | 1 |
| Turner, Percival Stanley<br>"Stan" or "The Bull"<br>F/O & F/L<br>Toronto, Ont.<br>*Awarded DFC October 8* | 242<br>Coltishall | Hurricanes | 2 | 1 | 1 |
| Walker, James<br>P/O & F/O<br>Gletchen, Alta. | 111<br>Drem & Kenley | Hurricanes | 2 | 0 | 0 |

| Name | Squadron / Base | Aircraft | | | |
|---|---|---|---|---|---|
| Walker, James Richard<br>P/O<br>Onoway, Alta. | 41<br>Hornchurch | Spitfires | 1 1/2 | 0 | 0 |
| Wallace, Clarence<br>P/O<br>Vancouver, B.C.<br>*Member of RCAF attached to RAF* | 3<br>Turnhouse | Hurricanes | 0 | 0 | 0 |
| Walsh, John<br>"Jack"<br>Bassano, Alta. | 615<br>Turnhouse & Northolt | Hurricanes | 0 | 0 | 0 |
| Ward, Rufus<br>Sgt-Pilot<br>*Only Canadian NCO in the Battle of Britain* | 66<br>Biggin Hill | Spitfires | 0 | 1 | 2 |
| Waterton, William Albert<br>P/O<br>Edmonton, Alta. | 242<br>Coltishall | Hurricanes | 0 | 0 | 0 |
| Watson, Frederick<br>Flt/Sgt<br>Winnipeg, Man.<br>*Member of RCAF attached to RAF* | 3<br>Wick | Hurricanes | 0 | 0 | 0 |

| | Squadron | Flying | Destroyed | Probably Destroyed | Damaged |
|---|---|---|---|---|---|
| Wilson, Robert "Ray" P/O Moncton, N.B. *Killed in action August 11* | 111 Drem & Kenley | Hurricanes | 1 | 0 | 0 |
| Yuile, Arthur F/O Montreal, P.Q. | 1 RCAF Northolt | Hurricanes | 1 | 0 | 1 |

# III/BRIEFING ON SOURCES

In relating the role of Canadians in the Battle of Britain, I relied heavily on several published sources as well as combat reports, biographical files, RCAF records, and official correspondence and records.

Hugh Halliday's *Canadians in the Battle of Britain* — a section of the Canadian Aviation Historical Society's *I'll Never Forget* — provides every single victory by pilot and date, type of aircraft attacked, squadrons and other detail such as wounded or killed in action. In addition, Halliday's *The Canadian Years*, although essentially a history of 242 Squadron, is a useful source of material and background about Canadians who joined the RAF in the 1930s, prior to World War II.

*The Narrow Margin* by Derek Wood and Derek Dempster is as complete a study of the Battle of Britain as has been written. It is a day-by-day account that provides such details as weather, targets, number of aircraft in the air and losses, as well as strategy and tactics on both sides. It also gives Allied and German squadron dispositions by airfield locations and type of aircraft flown.

Dave McIntosh's *High Blue Battle*, something of a classic, is a history of No. 1 Fighter Squadron RCAF (later 401 Squadron). It describes a day-by-day account, a slightly abridged version of the squadron diary during the Battle of Britain.

These are my principal references. My interpretation of them is my own, for which I make no apology.

Arthur Bishop
Raccoon Terrace
Toronto, January 1994

# BIBLIOGRAPHY

Angelucci, E., and P. Matricardi. *Combat Aircraft of World War II*. Vol. 3. New York: The Military Press, 1987.

Bader, Douglas. *Fight for the Sky*. Glasgow: Fontana/Collins, 1973.

Barker, A.J. *Stuka 87*. London: Bison Books, 1980.

Barker, Ralph. *The RAF at War*. Alexandria, VA: Time-Life Books, 1981.

————. *The Schneider Trophy Races*. London: Chatto & Windus, 1971.

Batchelor, John, and Bryant Cooper. *Fighter: A History of Fighter Aircraft*. New York: Ballantine Books, 1973.

Bishop, Arthur. *Courage in the Air: Canada's Military Heritage*. Vol. 1. Toronto: McGraw-Hill Ryerson Ltd., 1992.

Bishop, Edward. *Their Finest Hour*. New York: Ballantine Books, 1968.

Brickhill, Paul. *Reach for the Sky*. New York: Collins, 1954.

Caidin, Martin. *Me 109*. New York: Ballantine Books, 1968.

Churchill, Winston. *Their Finest Hour*. Boston: Houghton Mifflin Co., 1949.

Collier, Basil. *The Battle of Britain*. London: B.T. Batsford Ltd., 1962.

Craig, James F. *The Messerschmitt Bf 109*. New York: Arco Publishing Co. Inc., 1968.

Deighton, Len. *Fighter*. London: Jonathan Cape, 1977.

————. *Battle of Britain*. Toronto: Clarke, Irwin, 1980.

Galland, Adolf. *The First and the Last*. New York: Ballantine Books, 1957.

Halliday, Hugh. *The Canadian Years*. Stittsville, Ont.: Canada's Wings Inc., 1981.

————. *I'll Never Forget: Canadians in the Battle of Britain*. Published by the Canadian Aviation Historical Society.

Houton, Ted. *Spitfire Special*. London: Ian Allan Ltd., 1972.

Johnson, J.E. *Full Circle*. New York: Ballantine Books, 1964.

Kent, J.A. *One of the Few*. London: William Kimber and Co. Ltd., 1971.

Killen, John. *The History of the Luftwaffe*. New York: Berkley Medallion Books, 1967.

Kostenuk, Samuel, and John Griffin. *RCAF Squadron Histories and Aircraft*. Toronto: A.M. Hakkert Ltd., 1977.

Mason, Herbert Moiloy, Jr. *The Rise of the Luftwaffe*. New York: Ballantine Books, 1973.

McIntosh, David. *High Blue Battle*. Toronto: Stoddart, 1990.

Milberry, Larry, and Hugh Halliday. *The Royal Canadian Air Force at War, 1939-1945*. Toronto: Canav Books, 1990.

Milberry, Larry. *Sixty Years*. Toronto: Canav Books, 1984.

Price, Alfred. *Spitfire*. London: Macdonald & Janes Publishers Ltd., 1977.
————. *Spitfire at War*. London: Ian Allan Ltd., 1974.
Royal Air Force Association. *Against All Odds*. London, 1990.
Royal Canadian Air Force Historical Section. *The RCAF: The First Four Years*. Toronto: Oxford University Press, 1944.
Schirer, William. *The Rise and Fall of the Third Reich*. New York: Simon & Schuster, 1960
Townsend, Peter. *Duel of Eagles*. New York: Simon & Schuster, 1971.
Vader, John. *Spitfire*. New York: Ballantine Books, 1969.
Wallace, Graham. *RAF Biggin Hill*. London: Putnam & Co. Ltd., 1969.
Wells, H.G. *The Outline of History*. New York: Garden City Books, 1949.
Winterbotham, F.W. *The Ultra Secret*. New York: Dell, 1974.
Wood, Derek, and Derek Dempster. *The Narrow Margin*. London: Arrow Books, 1961.
Wright, Robert. *Dowding and the Battle of Britain*. London: Macdonald & Co., 1969.

# Index of Names and Squadrons

# ABOUT THE AUTHOR

Arthur Bishop enlisted in the Royal Canadian Air Force in 1941 and served overseas as a fighter pilot with 401 Squadron, flying Spitfires. After the war he joined the *Windsor Star* as a reporter and then began a career with Ronalds Advertising Agency, where he became a senior partner, director and vice-president. In 1967, he formed PPS Publicity Ltd., a public relations firm serving many of Canada's leading corporations. He is past director of the Canadian Fighter Pilots Association as well as the Canadian International Air Show.

Bishop is the author of *Courage in the Air*, *Courage on the Battlefield*, and *Courage at Sea*. He also wrote a biography of his father, World War I ace William (Billy) Avery Bishop, titled *The Courage of the Early Morning*, soon to be made into a feature film.